D1097351

THE EXCELLENT PATH TO ENLIGHTENMENT

THE EXCELLENT PATH TO ENLIGHTENMENT

Short Preliminary Practice
by
Jamyang Khyentse Wangpo

Explained
by
H.H. Dilgo Khyentse Rinpoche

Translated from the Tibetan

December, 1987

DISTRIBUTED BY:

Shechen Tennyi Dargyeling
Buddhist Monastery,
P.O BOX 136 Kathmandu, NEPAL.

Shechen Tennyi Dargyeling, Inc.
2nd Floor, 36 W 20 St, New York,
NY 10011 USA.

Shechen Tennyi Dargyeling Foundation,
La Sonnerie, 24290 Montignac,
FRANCE.

Rangjung Yeshey, Kanying Shedrup Ling,
P.O BOX 1200, Kathmandu, NEPAL.

This book was electronically typeset in
Bitstream's Palatino typeface
by the Nalanda Translation Committee
616 Alpine Ave., Boulder, CO 80302, U.S.A.

CONTENTS

The General Preliminaries   1

1) The contemplation of the rarity
   and preciousness of a human birth   2
2) The contemplation of death
   and impermanence   5
3) The contemplation of karma,
   the law of cause and effect   8
4) The contemplation of suffering   11
5) The contemplation of the unsur-
   passable qualities of liberation   13
6) The contemplation of the need
   to follow a spiritual master   14

The Extraordinary Preliminaries   19

Taking refuge   19
Bodhicitta   29
Vajrasattva   45
Mandala Offering   57
Guru Yoga   79

Notes   86

Text and Outline of the practice   89

THE EXCELLENT PATH TO ENLIGHTENMENT

In order to listen to the teachings, we must first generate the proper attitude as all the scriptures of the Sutras and Tantras explain. Mainly, this implies our having the great aspiration to achieve Enlightenment for the sake of others. The Buddha gave a vast number of teachings intended for beings of different capacities. Of all these, we will explain here the instructions called the *preliminary* or *foundation practice* which has two parts: the outer or general part and the inner or extraordinary part.

The General Preliminaries

To start with, knowing that devotion is the main source of our progress on the path, at the beginning of each session we should visualize in the sky before us, or above our head, our root guru in the form of Guru Padmasambhava, resplendent with wisdom, smiling with compassion, seated in the midst of a mass of rainbow light. Then with strong devotion we say three times, "*Lama kyeno!*", which may be rendered: "Guru you know everything! I am in your hands!", and ask him to bless us so that we may achieve complete realization of the profound path in this very life. Rays of light emanate from the Guru, clearing away the veil of ignorance and filling us with blessings.

We then reflect on the outer or general part of these preliminaries, for which there are six topics. The first is to reflect upon the rarity of human existence, which will cause our minds to turn towards the Dharma. The second is the contemplation of death and impermanence, which makes us realize how urgent it is to practice the Dharma and spur our endeavor. The third is to reflect on the law of karmic cause and effect, or actions and their results, which will lead us to a clear understanding of the way this law works. The fourth is the instruction to help us recognize that the deluded condition of samsara is never without suffering. The fifth is to recognize that through receiving and practicing the teachings, we can free ourselves from samsara and ultimately reach the unsurpassable level of omniscience, or Enlightenment. The sixth is to recognize that in order to achieve such a level we have to rely on the blessings and instructions of a spiritual teacher.

1) The contemplation of the rarity and preciousness of a human birth:

Ask yourself how many of the billions of inhabitants of this planet realize how rare it is to have been born a human being. How many of those who realize this think of using this chance to practice the Dharma? How many of these actually start to practice? How many of those who start continue to practice?

How many of those who continue attain ultimate realization? The number of those who attain ultimate realization is like the number of stars you can see at daybreak as opposed to the number of stars you can see on a clear night.

There can be various kinds of human existences. Some are wasted in ordinary pursuits and some are used to progress towards Enlightenment. Human birth can be called precious when one is free to practice the Dharma and has met all the favorable conditions for doing so. So to be free from the *eight unfavorable conditions* of which we will speak later gives us the opportunity to practice the Dharma. But leisure is not enough. We also need *ten favorable conditions*, five that depend upon ourselves and five that depend on others.

The five *intrinsic conditions* arising from our own situation are: to be born a human being, to be in a place where the Dharma can be found, to have all of one's faculties, not to live and act in a completely negative way, and to have faith in those worthy of faith.

We need to be born a human being, as this is the only state of existence in which there is enough suffering to make us wish intensely to be free of samsara, yet not so much suffering that we no longer have the opportunity to free ourselves through the practice of Dharma.

We need to be born in what is called a "*central land*", meaning a place where the Buddha's teachings exist. Otherwise we have no chance of meeting these teachings and progressing along the path.

We need all our faculties to study, reflect and practice the Dharma. If one were blind, for instance, one would not be able to read the teachings; if one were deaf, one would not be able to hear them.

We need to lead our life in a positive way. If the direction our life takes is towards negative actions - like being a hunter, a thief, or spending one's life in warfare - that naturally leads in the opposite direction from the positive conditions for Dharma.

We need to have faith and confidence in those who can guide us along the path to Enlightenment - the Three Jewels, and a spiritual teacher.

The five *external conditions* that depend upon others are: a Buddha must have appeared in the kalpa or aeon in which we are living, the Buddha must have taught the Dharma, the Dharma must still be present in our time, it must be practiced, and we must be guided by a spiritual teacher.

All this constitutes a human birth endowed with all the freedoms and favorable conditions for practicing the Dharma. That is what we call a *precious human* birth. Why is it precious? Because, using this human birth, there is a way to achieve Enlightenment in this very lifetime. All the great siddhas of the past were born ordinary beings; but, entering the door of the Dharma, following a realized teacher and devoting their whole lives to practicing the instructions they received, they could manifest the enlightened activities of great Bodhisattvas.

4

If we examine the six realms of samsara one by one, we can see that, except in the human realm, the obstacles to Dharma practice are too strong. In the inferior realms, like the hells, suffering is so intense that there is no chance for the mind to contemplate and practice the teachings. In the celestial realms, where beings can fly in the sky, feed on ambrosia and enjoy all sorts of pleasures, the conditions seem more favorable. But because these beings' minds are completely distracted by those enticements and their suffering is so minimal, they never get tired of samsara and therefore never think of practicing the Dharma. So, if we do not use the precious opportunity of a human existence, we have no choice but to go downhill like a rolling stone.

2) The contemplation of death and impermanence:

To have attained this human birth is not enough; we may lose it at any moment because of death. The time when death will come and the circumstances that will bring death are utterly uncertain. No one can say, "I will live this or that number of years and months." Any of the everyday circumstances of our daily life, like walking, eating, playing, crossing a river and so forth, could turn out to be the cause of our death.

Impermanence affects not only living beings but the outer universe as well. The world seems very solid to us, but at the end of the kalpa it will be destroyed by fire and water. Throughout the seasons of the year, one can see how the mountains, forests, and the various features of the landscape change from day to day, from month to month. Within each hour of every day, the weather, the light - everything changes. The river that flows before one's eyes is never the same, it changes as each instant goes by. Nations are powerful for a period of their history and later are conquered by other nations. Within the span of one lifetime, people can be very rich at one time and extremely poor and destitute at another. So, there is no certainty or permanence to any aspect of the outer phenomenal world.

Why do we need to reflect over and over again about impermanence? We have a strong tendency to think that we and all the conditions in which we are living will last, to think that there is some inherent permanence in them. Because of this, we generate very strong clinging to outer phenomena. This is a mistake. If, instead, we reflect constantly upon impermanence, we will develop a strong incentive for turning to the Dharma. We must constantly be aware that from the very moment we are born we come closer and closer to death. There is no way to avoid death. With every day that passes, our lives are running out. When the time of death comes, even if one is very powerful, there is no way to persuade death to wait. Even if one is very rich, one cannot bribe it. Even if one is a mighty general, one cannot send an army against it. If one is very beautiful, one cannot seduce death. There is no way one can stop death.

At the moment of death, nothing but the Dharma will be of any use. Of all fears encountered in this life there is none greater than death. So to be ready for death, we should not wait until the last moment to practice the Dharma. If we want to practice the Dharma now, we can; but at the time of death, we won't be able to. We will be overwhelmed by physical suffering and mental anguish. That is not the time to start thinking of practice. So, just as an intelligent person plans ahead, we should get ready right now to face death with the firmness of mature practice. We must not waste a single moment, like a warrior with a weapon stuck in his heart who knows that he has only a few moments to live. So it is now, while we are in good health and enjoy all our physical and mental faculties, that we should practice the Dharma. We must not postpone it, thinking, "I shall practice some time later." We must realize that death is a very frightful event for those who are not prepared for it. We must not think, "I have so many years ahead of me": the food we have just eaten could turn out to be poisonous and cause us to die tonight. There are many examples of unexpected causes of death. We can see them all around us.

Impermanence can be found in all aspects of life. People who have reached high positions can soon find themselves in lowly ones; many of those who have amassed a lot of money will later lose it - no-one remains wealthy forever. Those who have formed strong attachments to family and friends will sooner or later be separated from them, some now and all of them at the time of death. If we are aware of the constant threat of death, we will not want to continue the meaningless activities that we have engaged in, so heedlessly, day after day.

3) *The contemplation of karma, the law of cause and effect:*

If death were simply like a fire going out or like water drying up, it would be fine. It would then be of little use to practice the Dharma. But this is not the case. When the mind and body separate, the body is left behind, but the mind will take many more rebirths. At that point, the only thing that will determine the direction that our existence will take is the balance of the positive and negative actions that we have committed in the past and are embedded in our consciousness. If negative actions predominate, we will experience the suffering of rebirth in the lower realms. If positive ones predominate, we will experience rebirth in the higher states of existence. It is not on our deathbed or in the bardo[1] that we should start to think about positive and negative actions. We may very well recognize at that time that negative actions are the cause of our suffering, and that positive actions are what would lead us to happiness. But at the time of death there is nothing much we can do - our karma has already been built up.

It is now, when we have the freedom to choose between what we should do and what we should not do, that we must consider the law of karma. If we think that we may do whatever pleases us, good or bad, and that by practicing a little Dharma on the side we will be taken to Enlightenment as though in an airplane, that is a serious mistake.

In the bardo, even if we regret all our negative actions, we are just like a stone that has been thrown into the air; it can only fall down. We cannot reverse the process - karma has been accumulated. It is too late. So it is now that we must have a fine discrimination in recognizing positive and negative actions. Even if a positive action seems insignificant, we must do it. Even if a negative action seems minute, we must avoid it. Water dripping for a long time can fill a huge basin; likewise, every action has its result. One should never think that a minor action leaves no trace.

However, even if we have engaged in negative actions, we should not think that they mark us forever. Whatever the weight of our negative actions may be, they can be purified. There is nothing that cannot be purified. So we must regret and repair all our negative actions. As we said, just as small drops of water can fill a huge vessel, throughout our daily life we must constantly endeavor to gather positive actions through our body, speech and mind. This will build up an accumulation of merit and virtue that will help us when faced with the fear of death. The magnitude of positive and negative actions does not depend upon their outer aspects. It is easy to accumulate great positive karma or great negative karma with a small action. It all depends upon our intention or attitude. For instance, to help someone in a small way, but with great loving kindness, will accumulate a lot of positive karma. Likewise, a simple word is very easy to say, but if that word is, for instance, criticism of a Bodhisattva, it will accumulate boundless negative karma.

The general condition of beings in samsara is delusion, a state that always produces suffering. So if we just leave our negative actions alone, without purifying them, without confessing and repairing them, then gradually we will accumulate negative karma. We will not be able to receive the blessings of the

9

Buddhas and spiritual teachers; we will not be able to develop spiritual experience and realization. So we must constantly be aware and mindful of the difference between virtuous and nonvirtuous actions, cultivating the former while avoiding the latter.

When you wake up in the morning, think: "I have the good fortune to have been born as a human being. Not only that; I have entered the door of the Dharma, met a spiritual teacher, and received his instructions. So today I shall do my best to follow the Dharma and practice only what is positive. This I shall do not only for my own sake, but for the benefit of all living beings without a single exception."

When it is time to rest in the evening, examine the actions, words and thoughts that you have experienced during the day. If you have done something positive for yourself or others, you should rejoice, dedicate the merit to all sentient beings and pray that by this merit they may all attain Enlightenment. Wish that the next day you may cultivate even more virtuous actions. If you realize that you have fallen into negative deeds, think: "I have this precious human birth, I have met a teacher, and yet I am behaving in this way." You must feel strong regret and determination not to make such mistakes again.

To acquire mindfulness one needs constantly to examine one's intentions and actions. Ordinary beings who go round and round in samsara do not even think that their negative actions are negative - that they will bring harmful consequences. Even if they do think that for a short while, they do not keep it in mind, and hardly any of them put into action the means to counter these negative actions. This is the very reason why they stay in samsara. So one needs acute and diligent mindfulness of one's intentions and actions. For that one needs, first, to remember clearly which actions should be avoided and which should be carried out, and, second, to observe whether or not one is acting in accordance with what one knows to be right or wrong.

In order to develop diligent and steadfast mindfulness, we must realize that our condition, our suffering in samsara, is not the result of anything but our negative actions. If we do not stop these negative actions but just continue in the same way, we will continue to experience suffering. By cultivating positive actions, words and thoughts, we are earning our own happiness. If we know this, we will naturally watch over our mind with an alert diligence.

4) *The contemplation of suffering:*

What is the reason for cultivating virtue and avoiding non-virtue? The nature of the ordinary samsaric condition is nothing but suffering. This will become clear if one looks at the various realms of samsara. In the hell realms there is unbearable suffering due to heat or cold; the cause of this state of being is anger and hatred. The tortured spirits do not even hear of water and food for many years; the cause of this state is greed and miserliness. Animals are blind to the path of liberation and have no way of recognizing what will bring them happiness or suffering; domestic animals are used as slaves and slaughtered for their meat and skin; the cause of this state is stupidity, lack of discernment between virtue and nonvirtue. These are the three lower realms of samsara, each a most miserable condition.

There are also the three so-called higher realms - of the human beings, demi-gods and gods. Human beings have eight different types of suffering. They suffer birth, sickness, old age and death. They suffer when encountering enemies, parting from friends, meeting with conditions they do not want and being parted from the conditions they like.

Demigods are constantly tormented by jealousy and animosity towards the gods, or celestial beings, because the wish-fulfilling tree is rooted in their realm but bears its fruit in the realm of the gods. When the demi-gods see the gods enjoying this fruit, and also the lakes of ambrosia and all the other pleasures and perfections they cannot have themselves, they burn with unbearable jealousy and try to attack and fight the gods, but are always defeated.

Even the celestial beings, who seem to have everything one could desire - beautiful palaces, beautiful gardens, forests filled with flowers and birds, beautiful companions, delicious food and so forth - are far from being beyond suffering. Once they have enjoyed these fruits of minor positive actions and their karma has been exhausted, they will be reborn again in the most sorrowful states of samsara.

5) *The contemplation of the unsurpassable qualities of liberation:*

If you think about all the different states you can experience in samsara and realize there is nothing beyond suffering, strong feelings of weariness and sadness will arise. You will think, "How can I ever free myself from this suffering?" This is called the feeling of renunciation, the desire to get out of samsara, which is the very foundation on which one starts to practice the Dharma. If someone has been thrown into prison by a powerful king, he will think, day and night, "How miserable I am. How can I get out of here? Who can help me?" These will be his only thoughts. In the same way, once you recognize that conditions in samsara are unsatisfactory, and are nothing but suffering, you will think, "How can I achieve liberation? Who can help me? What are the means of obtaining liberation?" When you think very deeply about this, it will become clear that you need the help of a spiritual teacher, that you must avoid the kind of actions that lead to suffering, and that you must cultivate those that bring happiness. This is the way to tread the path of the Dharma.

Yet to cross the threshold of the Dharma does not mean to adopt all sorts of outer attitudes and signs; it means to become aware of the shortcomings and endless misery of samsara and of the unchanging qualities of liberation.

Otherwise, if we fail to recognize the suffering inherent in samsara, since we lack the incentive to get out of it, we may find the teachings interesting, but will be more concerned about how to increase our wealth, how to gain a higher position, more power and so forth. With such motivation, even if we do what seems to be a good action, it has little strength for freeing ourself and others from samsara.

You must realize that, just like yourself, all living beings are subject to suffering. Have the courage to think, "I have to be able to free all sentient beings by myself. In order to do this, the first step is to free myself, to achieve perfection and attain Enlightenment." This must be the root motivation for practicing the Dharma. With such an attitude, you will gradually deepen your spiritual experience, achieve realization and thus become truly able to help other beings.

6) *The contemplation of the need to follow a spiritual master*

Parents, friends and ordinary teachers cannot help one achieve liberation, for they are not free from samsara themselves. To attain Enlightenment one must have the guidance of an authentic spiritual master. Without a spiritual master one would get nowhere, like a passenger in an airplane without a pilot. So do not overestimate your capacities. Having searched and found a qualified master endowed with wisdom, compassion and ability, follow him with confidence, receive his instructions and practice them with diligence.

The contemplation of these six topics, and the practices that follow, are commonly known as *ngondro*, "preliminary practices," but when we say "preliminary," we are not implying that these are practices of lesser importance. A sound foundation is the foremost requirement in building a solid house. The same is true of Dharma practice. To practice the *ngondro* is not simply to accumulate numbers, even though one does one hundred thousand prostrations and the same number of recitations of each of the five *ngondro* sections. The real point of *ngondro* is to appreciate that this human life offers a rare opportunity for one to achieve liberation, to realize the urgency of doing so, to generate a strong conviction that the ordinary samsaric condition produces only suffering, and to realize that suffering comes about through karma - the effect of negative actions. If these four understandings really take birth in one's being, then the main point of *ngondro* has been realized. You should not only think about them, but experience them in your being. True foundation practice is when this has become a part of oneself.

Do not think that the *ngondro* is some kind of lowly or beginner's practice or that it is not as profound as *Mahamudra*, the Great Seal, or *Ati Yoga*, the Great Perfection. In fact, *ngondro* practice comes at the beginning precisely because it is of crucial importance and is the very ground of all other practices. If we were to go straight to the so-called "main practice" without the preparation of the *ngondro*, it would not help us at all, because our mind would be untamed and unprepared. It would be like building a beautiful house on the surface of a frozen lake - something that won't last!

The purpose of generating a strong feeling of renunciation or disgust with samsara is to lead one gradually to the state of Buddhahood. Dharma practice is a little difficult in the beginning but becomes easier and easier as one goes along. Worldly activities are very easy and enjoyable at the start but bring more and more suffering in the long run.

In all the steps of the practice, we must always keep clearly in mind that we are practicing for the sake of all sentient beings. "All" sentient beings is not a certain number, since the number of sentient beings is boundless and infinite, like the sky. If we dedicate each one of our actions to the welfare of all beings, the benefit of these actions will remain and grow until we achieve Enlightenment. The aspiration to practice for the sake of all others is in fact the very root of achieving Enlightenment.

Ngondro practice includes the recitation of some verses. Here, for this first part, recite the following:

> *Lama kyeno!*
>
> *Now that I possess these freedoms and endowments, so difficult to obtain, and of such importance,*
> *May I arouse my mind by remembering the impermanence of the universe and beings.*
> *To free myself truly from the ocean of suffering of the three worlds[2].*
> *Without confusing what is to be adopted and what is to be abandoned, may I persevere in the path.*

In some other *ngondro* practices, the *Longchen Nyingthig Ngondro* for instance, the text to be recited goes into far more detail than this. In either case, the recitation on its own will not help very much. While reciting we must constantly be aware of the meaning

16

and intention of the text. What must change is the way we perceive the outer world. We must become truly convinced that the ordinary state of samsara is nothing but suffering. We must constantly keep in mind impermanence, the relentless passage of time, and the imminence of death. We need to be careful of our actions and should never dismiss the law of karma, cause and effect, as unimportant. We must recognize the need to achieve liberation and the need to rely upon a spiritual teacher in order to do so. Then the meaning of the teachings will truly become a part of ourself. This is very important.

18

The Extraordinary Preliminaries

TAKING REFUGE

The inner part of the *ngondro*, or preliminary practice, starts with the teachings on refuge, the gateway to the path.

In whom do we take refuge? In the Three Jewels, the "Three Rare and Supreme Ones," the Buddha, the Dharma and the Sangha. It is important to recognize the value of these Three Jewels.

The first Jewel is the Buddha. His qualities are displayed in the three kayas: the *Dharmakaya* or absolute body, the *Sambhogakaya* or body of perfect enjoyment, and the *Nirmanakaya* or manifested body. The Dharmakaya expresses itself as five wisdoms: the wisdom of the absolute expanse, the mirror-like wisdom, the wisdom of equality, the all-distinguishing wisdom, and the wisdom of all-accomplishing action. These five wisdoms appear as the Sambhogakaya Buddhas of the five families, who continually turn the wheel of Dharma in the Buddhafields for their perfect retinue of Bodhisattvas; they manifest in forms perceptible to ordinary beings, the Nirmanakaya Buddhas such as the Buddha Shakyamuni.

The second Jewel is the Dharma, the expression of the Buddha's wisdom for the sake of all sentient beings.

The third Jewel is the Sangha, which is composed of all those who practice the path shown by the Buddha.

There is an inner aspect to the Three Jewels, known as the Three Roots: the Guru who is the root of blessing, the Yidam who is the root of accomplishment and the Dakini who is the root of enlightened activity. Although the names are different, these three in no way differ from the Three Jewels. The Guru is the Buddha, the Yidam is the Dharma, and the Dakinis and Protectors are the Sangha. And at the innermost level, the Dharmakaya is the Buddha, the Sambhogakaya is the Dharma and the Nirmanakaya is the Sangha.

To take refuge, we visualize an object of refuge in front of us. We should not perceive the outer environment as the ordinary or "impure" world, but as a pure Buddhafield which has all the perfections, wish-fulfilling trees, lakes of nectar, golden ground and jewel mountains. All sounds there, even the songs of the birds and the rustling of the leaves, are the sound of mantras and praises of the Buddhas. The mere taste of the nectar-like water engenders deep states of meditation. In the center of this Buddhafield, visualize an immeasurable wish-fulfilling tree, in full bloom, made of precious substances: the trunk and branches of jewels, the leaves of gold, and the fruits and flowers of different kinds of precious gems. Between the branches hang garlands of coral, pearls, amber, turquoise and so forth. There are tiny bells, their clear tones voicing the teachings of Dharma.

The tree has a central trunk and four main branches. Upon the central trunk is a throne made of various sorts of jewels and supported by eight fearless lions. On the throne is a multicolored lotus, and on the lotus are a sun disc and a moon disc. Upon the moon disc, seated in a luminous expanse of rainbow light, smiling radiantly, full of wisdom and compassion, is our root teacher - the one to whom we have the strongest natural devotion - in the form of the precious Lotus-Born Guru, Guru Rinpoche.

Above in the sky, starting from the primordial Buddha Samantabhadra down to Guru Rinpoche himself, are, one below the other, all the teachers of the lineage of the three transmissions, and, to the sides, all the great teachers of the Nyingma, Kagyu, Sakya, and Geluk lineages to whom one feels devotion.

Of the four main branches, on the front branch is Buddha Shakyamuni, surrounded by the one thousand and two Buddhas of this fortunate aeon, dressed in the three monastic robes, ablaze with the glory of the thirty-two major and eighty minor marks of an enlightened Buddha, such as the protuberance on the crown of the head, the wheel pattern on the palms of the hands and soles of the feet, and so forth.

On the right branch are the heart-sons of the Buddha, the eight great Bodhisattvas, - Manjushri, Avalokiteshvara, Vajrapani and so forth - and all the other Bodhisattvas of the Mahayana, the Great Vehicle. They are beautifully adorned with the five silken

21

garments[3] and the eight jeweled ornaments[4] of the Sambhogakaya. They are standing, facing forward, ready to benefit beings.

On the left branch is the noble community, the Sangha of the Hinayana, led by Shariputra and Maudgalyayana, the two principal disciples of Lord Buddha, and comprising the sixteen Arhats, the eight great Sthaviras and all the Sangha of the Hinayana, sitting in different meditative postures, holding begging bowl and mendicant's staff.

On the rear branch are all the scriptures of the three vehicles, beautifully arranged on a jeweled shrine, their titles facing us. They spontaneously emanate the sounds of the Sanskrit vowels and consonants, as well as the teachings of the Prajnaparamita and all of the Mahayana sutras. These scriptures symbolize both the *Dharma of transmission*, the written teachings themselves, and the *Dharma of realization*, the qualities of Enlightenment.

All around in the sky and in between the branches, like masses of clouds, are the Herukas of the six classes of Tantras, as well as the Dakas, Dakinis and Protectors of the Dharma. The male Protectors, like Gonpo Maning, Lekden, the Four-Armed Mahakala, the Six-Armed Mahakala, the guardian of Samye (Dorje Lekpa), Rahula, and others, face outwards to ward off obstacles to our practice; the female Protectors, such as Ekajati, Tseringma and the others, face inwards to prevent the blessings and accomplishments from being lost to the outside.

All these deities and spiritual teachers fill the whole of space, just like bees swarming from a hive as it is breaking open. They should be visualized very clearly, transparent and vivid, as though made of rainbow light, radiating wisdom, compassion and strength.

We consider ourself to be standing in front of the object of the object of refuge, facing it. On our right is our father in this life. On our left is our mother. Behind and at the sides are all beings of the six realms, and in front are all those whom we perceive as our enemies. As if we were leading them, with the body we show respect by all prostrating together towards the object of refuge; with speech we recite the verses for taking refuge; and with mind we generate complete confidence and faith in the objects of refuge.

We must take refuge with the vast attitude of the Mahayana, taking refuge not only for this lifetime, but until we attain Enlightenment - not only for our own sake, but for the sake of establishing all sentient beings in Enlightenment.

The verse one actually recites is:

Homage!
Until the Enlightenment of myself and all beings,
I take refuge in the Three Roots.

Recite the refuge prayer one hundred thousand times while doing the same number of prostrations (in practice, as explained in the instructions with the root text, we recite here the four-line verse which also includes the two lines on Bodhicitta.)

23

At the end of each session, we visualize rays of wisdom light emanating from the entire object of refuge, touching ourself and all sentient beings, purifying all our suffering and obscurations and causing wisdom to be born in our mind. Then ourself and all sentient beings take flight towards the refuge, like when a stone is thrown into the middle of a flock of birds, and we all dissolve into Guru Rinpoche. Then the gurus, yidams, dakinis and protectors melt into light and dissolve into Guru Rinpoche, who becomes even more radiant, sitting in space, dazzling, the union of all Buddhas. Finally, like a rainbow vanishing in the sky, Guru Rinpoche himself dissolves into void, luminous space. Remain for some time in this state.

This expanse of void luminosity is nothing but the nature of one's mind. Remaining in that state of utter simplicity will bring one to the realization that the void nature of mind is the Dharmakaya; that its expression, luminosity or wisdom, is the Sambhogakaya; and that its manifestation, all-pervading compassion, is the Nirmanakaya. One will realize that the object of refuge, the Three Jewels, is nothing outside oneself, but is naturally present within one's mind. This is the ultimate refuge.

Three supreme methods must be applied to taking refuge, as well as to any other practice or action one may perform: first, one must prepare by wishing to practice for the sake of all sentient beings; second, one must concentrate fully on the practice itself; lastly, one must dedicate the merit for the sake of all beings.

Here the preparation is to take refuge for the benefit of all sentient beings. The main part is to take refuge with full concentration, having total confidence in the Buddha, Dharma and Sangha, and in the Guru, the Yidam deity and the Dakinis. Confidence means that even if one suffers from heat or cold, even if one is struck with illness, suffering or unhappiness. Here the preparation is to take refuge for the benefit of all sentient beings. The main part is to take refuge with full concentration, having total confidence in the Buddha, Dharma and Sangha, and in the Guru, the Yidam deity and the Dakinis. Confidence means that even if one suffers from heat or cold, even if one is struck with illness, suffering or unhappiness, one will always only rely on the Three Jewels and the Three Roots. Even at the cost of one's life, there is no way one renounces them. At that point one's taking refuge has become genuine.

Having taken refuge in the fully enlightened Buddha, one must not seek refuge in celestial beings, gods of wealth or power, elemental forces, spirits, stars, mountains and so forth, as none of these transcends samsara. As statues and paintings are the representations of the Buddha's form, one must treat these images with respect (even a broken piece of a statue), and place them in an elevated and clean place.

Having taken refuge in the Dharma, since the root of Dharma is the wish to benefit others, one must give up any form of violence towards other sentient beings. As the scriptures are the support of Dharma and can lead one to Enlightenment, one must never step over books[5], and one must even avoid stepping on any kind of writing, even a single letter of the alphabet, for it can form part of a Buddha's name. One must not treat written material in a casual way or put it in dirty places, but keep it in a high place, or, if one has to dispose of it, burn it in a clean place.

Having taken refuge in the Sangha, one should avoid associating with people whose views and ways of life are completely contrary to the Dharma. One should have confidence in and respect for the Sangha of the Hinayana, monks and nuns, and the sangha of the Mahayana, the Bodhisattvas.

In brief, the essence of taking refuge is to have complete confidence in the refuge, regardless of whether the circumstances one may encounter in one's life are good or bad. If one encounters pleasant or favorable circumstances, one should think that it is purely due to the kindness and blessings of the Three Jewels. One should be grateful and dedicate this happiness to all sentient beings, wishing that they too may enjoy such happiness. If one encounters difficult circumstances, becomes sick, destitute, or the object of criticism or derision, one should think that the misdeeds one has committed during countless past lives would normally cause one to be born in the lower realms of samsara; yet, by the kindness of the guru and the Three Jewels and by the strength of one's confidence in them, today, through experiencing sickness and difficulties, one has a chance to purify this karma to be reborn in the lower realms. One should also pray, "Through this suffering of mine, may I take on the suffering of all beings who are enduring similar difficulties. May this difficulty help me to progress on the path to Enlightenment."

One must maintain one's reliance on the refuge throughout all activities in daily life. For instance, at night, think that the object of refuge is dwelling above your head, bright and vivid, and fall asleep keeping your mind filled with devotion. When walking, think that the refuge is above your right shoulder and that you are walking around it respectfully. When eating, think that you are offering the first part of the food to the Three Jewels and then eat the rest as if it had been given back as a blessed substance. When you wear new clothes, first mentally offer them to the Three Jewels.

If you have complete confidence, it is not difficult for the blessings of the Three Jewels to reach you. If you do not, you close yourself to the blessings. The rays of the sun shine upon everyone in this world, but only by concentrating them through a magnifying glass can one set dry grass on fire. Likewise, if you have the magnifying glass of devotion, the Guru's blessings will blaze forth within you.

There are different levels of faith. First, when, hearing about the qualities of the Three Jewels and the lives of the Buddha and the great teachers, one's mind is filled with a clear joy and one's perceptions change, this is called *clear faith*. When thinking about them fills one with a great desire to know more about their qualities and to acquire them oneself, this is called *longing faith*. When, through practicing, one acquires complete confidence in the truth of the teachings and the Enlightenment of the Buddha, this is called *confident faith*. Finally, when faith has become so much a part of oneself that even at the cost of one's life there is no way one can give it up, it has transformed into *irreversible faith*. Faith is the overall foundation of Dharma practice. There is no practice, even Mahamudra or

Dzogchen[6], which is not supported by faith in the refuge. Refuge is both the foundation to start with and also, if one understands the deeper meaning of the refuge, it is the ultimate goal of realizing the Buddha within. Therefore, from now until Enlightenment, the refuge should be an integral part of one's practice.

BODHICITTA,
THE THOUGHT OF ENLIGHTENMENT

Bodhicitta is the thought of achieving Enlightenment for the sake of all beings. Two levels can be distinguished in the Buddhist teachings, the Lesser Vehicle, Hinayana, and the Great Vehicle, Mahayana. We are practicing according to the Great Vehicle. It is called "great" because of the greatness of its attitude and its intention, which is to include all sentient beings in the aspiration to achieve Enlightenment.

There are two levels of Bodhicitta: Absolute Bodhicitta and Relative Bodhicitta. Relative Bodhicitta also falls into two aspects or stages, which are Bodhicitta as aspiration and Bodhicitta as action.

Absolute Bodhicitta is the realization that the ultimate nature of all phenomena is emptiness. But this is not something that is easily understood in the beginning. So in order to realize Absolute Bodhicitta one needs first to cultivate Relative Bodhicitta.

To take the bodhisattva vow, to generate Bodhicitta, one needs a witness, such as one's teacher or an image of the Buddha. For this practice, one takes the Bodhisattva vow in front of Guru Rinpoche, surrounded by the refuge assembly as described earlier.

In front of the object of refuge, one visualizes oneself alone this time, because it is oneself who is making a promise, the promise to work for the sake of all beings. One recites:

> To obtain Buddhahood for the benefit of others,
> I generate Bodhicitta, as aspiration, as action, and
>   in its absolute meaning.

What is the essence of and need for Bodhicitta? Sentient beings circle endlessly in the three realms of samsara because of three obscurations: attachment or desire, aversion or hatred, and ignorance. Buddha Nature, *tathagatagarbha*, is naturally present in every sentient being, but beings fail to recognize it and fall into delusion. This is ignorance, the very root of samsara.

The chief manifestation of this ignorance is the ego, the thought of "I." Once such a thought has taken place, one then conceives of "my body, my mind, my name." But actually the thought of "I" posits the existence of something that does not exist at all.

We now have this aggregation of various elements which we call "the body." As long as body and mind remain together, the various sense-consciousnesses perceive outer phenomena: we can see forms, we can hear sounds, we can smell odors, we can taste flavors, we can feel objects. Conceiving of an ego, we cling to the concept of a self-existent individual. Perceiving the outer world, we cling to the concept of self-existent phenomena. While we are alive, the body and mind operate together. We also have a name. However, when we start examining these three - body, mind, and name - we can easily see that these are mere labels devoid of any intrinsic reality.

Let us take a look at the body first. It is made up of different components: skin, blood, bones, flesh and organs. Let us take these apart, putting the skin on one side, the bones on another, the blood, the organs, etc... each in a separate place. One cannot call the skin alone the body. One cannot call the blood alone the body. Likewise, none of these constituents alone can be referred to as the body itself. None of these can be said even to contain any kind of essential "body-ness." So the body is merely a label attached to an aggregation of disparate elements that remain together for a while, and not something which has a real existence of its own. There is no such entity as a body. Yet, because one believes it is "my body," one feels greatly attracted to what is pleasurable to it, and wants to avoid at all costs what is unpleasant for it.

One also clings to the notion of "my mind." But if one tries to search for this mind, one cannot find it anywhere. It is not located in the brain, in the heart, in the skin or anywhere else in the body. It has no particular shape: it is neither round, square, nor oblong. It has no particular color. It is neither solid nor diffuse. So again, "mind" is merely a name attached to endless thoughts which constantly follow one after the other, just as "rosary" is a name given to a hundred beads threaded together.

The same is true for the notion of "name." For instance, we say "man" to designate a human being. The word "man" is just made up of the letters "m," "a" and "n." But if we separate the "m," the "a" and the "n," the idea of "man," or human being, has totally disappeared.

Once this system of false imputations has taken root, there are some beings and things that we then consider to be ours - our relatives, our friends who do good things for us and to whom we feel strongly attached. We cannot bear to be separated from them even for a few moments. We are ready to do any kind of action, positive or negative, to please or defend them. This is called attachment or desire.

There are other beings whom we somehow perceive as causing us harm, and we decide that they are our enemies. We are ready to harm them, in return, as much as we can. This is called aversion or hatred.

When such ignorance as this pervades the whole mind, the conditions for endless wandering in samsara are gathered together. In fact, attachment and aversion are just a failure to recognize that "enemy" and "friend" are fleeting and highly unreliable concepts. We have been born countless times in samsara. In each of our births we have had parents, friends and enemies. There is no certainty at all about who might have been our parents, friends, or enemies in our past lives, or who will be in our lives to come. Our most deadly enemy in this life might be our child in our next life. Our parents in this life might be our enemies in the next. We have gone through innumerable lives, not only a few. In these lives we have had so many different parents, not always the same ones in each lifetime. So there is not a single sentient being in this universe who has not been our father or mother at some time or another. Therefore, to have strong aversion or attachment to any of them, to consider them as enemies or friends, is just senseless. This only arises because we lack the ability to see what has happened to all sentient beings throughout countless lives. We are utterly deluded.

When we see someone and think, "He is my enemy," that thought is just a projection of our mind. If someone were to call us a thief. or perhaps even attack us with a stick, anger would well up in our mind, we would go red in the face, and we might think, "I must fight back and hit him even harder than he has hit me." So, we pick up a bigger stick and rush at him. Anger is so strong that it can lead us to such extremes, but if we look at anger itself, it is just a thought. If we look at that thought there is really nothing to it: it has no shape, color, location, or any other characteristic. It is empty. To recognize the empty nature of mind is Absolute Bodhicitta.

If we reflect carefully we see that there is not the slightest reason to be angry when someone hits us. It would be ridiculous to be angry with the stick itself - but perhaps it is even more ridiculous to be angry with the person who hit us. He is a victim of his own mental poisons, and deserves all our compassion for all the extra suffering he is building up for himself by acting in such a way. How could we be angry with a sick person whose mind is so disturbed?

We must rid our mind completely of these exaggerated attachments and aversions. If we have considered someone up till now as our enemy, we should now wish to benefit him as much as we can. If we have been strongly attached to someone, we can continue to benefit him, but we do not need to be caught up in our attachment. We must make our feelings of love and compassion equal for all beings.

There is no enemy to fight; there are no friends to hang on to. All beings equally deserve our love and kindness, like our own parents. We should think of how grateful we ought to be to our parents. First of all, they gave us life. Then from an early age they fed us, dressed us, educated us and loved us. We should extend this feeling of gratitude to all the infinity of sentient beings. The mutual love between parents and children is something very natural. Even the fiercest animal, like a tigress, has great love for her cubs. She is ready to give her life to save them at any moment. Yet this is a very one-sided, limited love for only a few beings. We must feel this kind of love for all living beings.

There is nowhere in samsara which is beyond suffering. All sentient beings without exception, even the tiniest insect, want only happiness. Yet all they do is to perpetuate their own suffering. The reason for this is that sentient beings do not recognize negative actions as the cause of suffering and positive actions as the cause of happiness. Animals, out of a desire to be comfortable and happy, kill other animals for food. By doing this, they generate further suffering both for other animals and for themselves. A madman who sticks a knife in his body, or who stays in freezing places in the winter without clothes, is basically someone who wants happiness, but unwittingly does all sorts of things that bring suffering upon himself. Likewise, failing to recognize that the only way to achieve happiness is to increase their positive actions and give up their negative ones, sentient beings cause their own suffering. If we think about this, an intense compassion for all deluded beings will arise in our mind.

To have compassion for all sentient beings is still not enough. Compassion alone cannot help. One has to put it into practice and really help sentient beings. If someone has done well in life and takes care of his old parents he will be respected by everyone; but if he neglects his parents, people will despise him. In the same way, not to help all the infinite sentient beings who have been one's kind parents throughout countless lifetimes is infinitely more despicable. So we must be determined to do whatever will be of benefit for all beings.

If one wants to benefit others, giving them food, clothes and ordinary affection will help to some extent, but the benefit is limited and only temporary. One must find a way to help others that is absolute and unchanging. This is something that ordinary acts of kindness to one's family and friends cannot do. Only the Dharma can do that. The Dharma can help sentient beings to become free from the lower states of samsara, and ultimately it will enable them to achieve Enlightenment. Of course, in the beginning, in one's present state, one does not have the ability to help others that the Buddhas and Bodhisattvas, such as Manjushri and Avalokiteshvara, have; the very reason for practicing the Dharma is to achieve that ability. This is why one must follow a spiritual master, receive his teachings and put them into practice.

With diligence, strong confidence and devotion anyone can attain Buddhahood, even an insect. At the very beginning, we should have the unwavering confidence that we can attain Enlightenment. We should also have a vast, courageous mind, thinking that we will be able to bring all sentient beings to Enlightenment too. If we simply think, "May I be free from my difficulties, be protected from fears and enjoy comfort and happiness," only caring about ourselves, this is a very narrow attitude. We should wish for unlimited happiness for the unlimited number of beings. The only way to fulfill this wish is to practice the Dharma and attain Enlightenment. If, from the very beginning, one dedicates one's efforts to the welfare of all beings, one's practice will be immune to negative influences like anger and pride. Not only that, but its benefit will endure and be perpetuated from now on until the moment of Enlightenment.

One can practice with body, speech and mind. Of these three, the most important is the mind. Indeed, though to practice with the body, doing prostrations and circumambulations, and with the speech, reciting prayers and mantras, has some great benefits, unless the mind is thoroughly turned towards the Dharma, these benefits will be limited.

Take the object of refuge as your witness, and firmly make this promise: "From now on, I will not have a single selfish thought. Even when I recite a single time OM MANI PADME HUNG, I shall do it for the sake of all beings. When I have even a single thought of devotion to my teacher, that will also be for the sake of all beings." This promise to work for the sake of all sentient beings is called "Bodhicitta as aspiration". "Bodhicitta as action" is all the positive actions one does to fulfill that aspiration.

Bodhicitta has boundless benefits and very few dangers. Why? Because if one is practicing solely for the sake of all beings, one's motivation is so pure that it becomes invulnerable to obstacles and deviations. It is a profound and, at the same time, a simple practice. In essence, Bodhicitta is the aim to become enlightened in order to help others attain Enlightenment.

When we undertake the actual practice of Bodhicitta, we again recite 100,000 times the four lines which combine refuge and Bodhicitta (this time without doing prostrations), concentrating mainly on the meaning of the Bodhisattva vow. At the end of each session, we pray to the object of refuge in the sky before us: "May Bodhicitta take birth in my being just as it is present in the wisdom mind of Guru Rinpoche." Then ,from the outside towards the center, all the lineage teachers and deities melt into light and dissolve into Guru Rinpoche. Guru Rinpoche himself melts into light and dissolves into us. At that moment, think that Guru Rinpoche's fully manifested Bodhicitta has become inseparably united with your own mind. At the end, conclude by wishing, "If precious Bodhicitta has not taken birth in my being, may it take birth. If it has taken birth, may it never degenerate but increase more and more." We should remember that what created the main obstacle to our generating Bodhicitta in the past was the distinction we made between friends and enemies. When we realize that all beings have been our kind parents in the past, it is senseless to see them as enemies. It is equally senseless to be attached to friends. Not only in past and future lives, but within this lifetime, there are people who were once very close to us, but who later became our enemies. To cling rigidly to the concepts of friend and enemy does not make any sense. Once we have completely given up attachment on one hand and aversion on the other, just as a pair of scales with equal weights on each side remains balanced, we will have complete equanimity towards all sentient beings.

The four boundless qualities

There are four boundless qualities which one must cultivate in order to develop Bodhicitta: loving kindness, compassion, joy, and equanimity. Of these four, the most fundamental is boundless equanimity, the state in which we make no distinction between friend and enemy. This is where we should begin our meditation. Boundless equanimity leads to the wisdom of sameness, one of the natural wisdoms of an enlightened Buddha.

To illustrate how a Bodhisattva puts the welfare of others before his own, we may recall how in a past existence Lord Buddha took rebirth as a turtle in the ocean. A ship was wrecked and five sailors were thrown into the water. The turtle came to the surface and, speaking in human words, told them, "Get on my back. I will take you to dry land." With great difficulty the turtle carried the five sailors to the shore of an island. They were saved. But the turtle was completely exhausted and needed to rest on the beach. She fell asleep. While she was sleeping, eighty thousand small insects came and started to eat her body. She awoke in great pain. The turtle thought, "If I go into the water now, all these insects will die." So she decided to give her own flesh and blood to them. The eighty thousand insects and worms completely ate the turtle. At the moment she was about to die, since she was a great Bodhisattva, she made the aspiration, "When I finally become a fully enlightened Buddha, may these five sailors and eighty thousand insects be the first to whom I teach the Dharma, setting them on the path of Enlightenment." In accordance with this prayer, when the Buddha had attained Enlightenment, he came to the Deer Park in Sarnath near Varanasi, where the five excellent disciples, the five bhikshus for whom Lord Buddha Shakyamuni turned the wheel of Dharma for the first time, were those who had been the five sailors; and the eighty thousand celestial beings who attended this first teaching were those who had been the eighty thousand insects. This exemplifies ultimate compassion, the ability to put the welfare of others before one's own.

Loving kindness is wishing that happiness and the cause of happiness may be experienced by all sentient beings without exception. All beings long for happiness, but hardly any achieve it; so to wish them as much happiness as possible and to wish that they may find the cause of happiness is called "loving kindness." Loving kindness has immeasurable qualities. If we have this love deep within our being, we naturally benefit others; and there is no way that any kind of evil influence can harm us, as compassion is the most powerful weapon against negative forces. There is another story about when Lord Buddha, then a Bodhisattva, was born in the form of a king named "Power of Love." It happened that five fierce ogres, or *rakshasas*, came into his kingdom. They reached a place where there were some shepherds herding sheep and other animals. The *rakshasas* thought that they could easily kill them, as they usually did, with their sharp nails and teeth, which were like iron. But they could not do any harm to either the shepherds or the animals - they could not even inflict the slightest wound. They became very upset, saying, "What is the reason for this? Anywhere in the world we can easily kill anybody. But here we cannot even scratch your skin." The shepherds replied, "This is due to the power of our king, who meditates constantly upon loving kindness in his palace." The *rakshasas* were amazed to hear of such an exceptional being, and asked the shepherds if they could meet their king. So the shepherds took them to the king, who told them, "If you give up all your thoughts of harming living beings, and, instead, wish to help others, and dedicate all your actions and thoughts to others's welfare, you will rid yourselves of evil karma; you will progress throughout your lives towards liberation from suffering." At that moment, Bodhicitta, the wish to help others achieve liberation, took birth in those fierce *rakshasas*. So, in short, loving kindness is the wish that others will experience happiness and find the cause of this happiness.

Compassion is wishing that all beings without exception may be free from suffering and the cause of suffering. Compassion is the feeling that comes from contemplating the suffering of others, and the wish to do something about it. There are many realms other than just the human realm. The hell realms, for instance, are filled with endless suffering. If we imagine that our parents have fallen into these hell realms, and are being attacked and stabbed with thousands of weapons and burned with intense fire, we will feel a strong impulse to do something to relieve their suffering and rescue them from their torment. This is the basic feeling of compassion. Beings are suffering everywhere in samsara. They are suffering from burning and freezing in the hell realm, from thirst and hunger in the hungry ghost realm, from slavery and slaughter in the animal realm, from birth, old age, sickness and death in the human realm, from jealousy and fighting in the demi-god realm, and, in the god realm, from losing their pleasures and falling back into lower existences. If we reflect on all this, we will feel, "How good it would be if I could free them all from their suffering!"

Joy is when, seeing beings gifted with great qualities, learned, and enjoying happiness, fame or power, we think, "May they continue to have happiness and enjoy even more happiness!", instead of feeling uneasy and envious of their good fortune. Furthermore, we should pray that they may use their wealth and power to help other beings, to serve the Dharma and the Sangha, to make offerings, build monasteries, propagate the teachings and perform other worthwhile deeds. We should rejoice and wish, "May they not be separated from all their happiness and their advantages. May their happiness increase more and more, and may they use it for the sake of others and for the benefit of the doctrine."

So, pray that your being may be blessed with the birth of boundless equanimity, loving kindness, compassion, and joy - as boundless as in the mind of a Bodhisattva. If you pray in this way, genuine Bodhicitta will certainly grow within you.

These four qualities are boundless, or immeasurable, because their object, the totality of sentient beings, is boundless; their benefit, the welfare of all beings, is boundless; and their fruit, the qualities of Enlightenment, is boundless. They are immeasurable like the sky, and are the true root of Enlightenment.

In this as in any other practice, we must apply three supreme methods: to wish that what we are doing may benefit all beings; to do it with full concentration, maintaining the understanding of the void nature of all phenomena; and to conclude it with the dedication of its merit for the sake of all beings. This is the best way to please the Buddhas and Bodhisattvas; and it is the best way to develop meditative experience and realization, without falling prey to obstacles arising from anger, attachment or pride.

VAJRASATTVA

At the beginning of our practice we reflected on the rarity and preciousness of this human existence. To spur our endeavor we reflected upon impermanence. To increase our mindfulness we reflected on the way actions lead to their results. Finally, we saw how the ordinary condition of samsara is never beyond suffering, and realizing the unchanging benefit of liberation we understood the need to find and rely upon a spiritual teacher. Then we went into the main part of the preliminary practice, first crossing the threshold of the Buddhadharma by taking refuge in the Buddha, Dharma and Sangha. We then developed Bodhicitta, the wish to attain Enlightenment for the sake of others, the root of the Vehicle of the Bodhisattvas. Now, entering the Vajrayana, we come to the meditation and recitation on Vajrasattva (tib: Dorje Sempa) the purpose of which is to remove hindrances on our path to Enlightenment. These hindrances are the obscurations and negative actions we have accumulated in the past.

Vajrasattva is the sovereign, the lord of all the mandalas of the Vajrayana, or Diamond Vehicle. To meditate on Vajrasattva is the same as meditating upon all the Buddhas. Likewise, his hundred-syllable mantra is the quintessence of all mantras.

The main obstacles to progress along the path to Enlightenment are the obscurations that come from our past negative actions. There are various kinds of negative actions. Some, like killing, stealing, lying or cheating are obviously intrinsically unvirtuous. Others are transgressions of vows and precepts taught by the Buddha or one's teacher for the sake of one's spiritual progress.

The main purpose of Vajrasattva practice is to purify these obscurations. It is said, "The only virtue of sin is that it can be purified." In fact, there is nothing that cannot be purified, even what may seem to be a negative deed of boundless magnitude.

The four strengths

In order to purify negative actions completely, one needs four strengths or forces: the strength of support, the strength of regret, the strength of the antidote, and the strength of the promise.

In order to purify oneself, one needs support for expressing one's remorse, offering one's confession and repairing the effects of one's past negative actions. In this case, the support is Vajrasattva. We visualize him above our head, utterly peaceful and smiling, brilliant white like a dazzling snow mountain illuminated by the rays of a hundred thousand suns. He sits in full vajra posture, upon a thousand-petaled white lotus and a moon disc. In his right hand he holds a golden vajra at his heart center; in his left, a silver bell resting at his hip. He is adorned with the thirteen Sambhogakaya adornments - the five silken garments and the eight jeweled ornaments. Vajrasattva is in union with his consort, Vajratopa[7], who in her right hand holds a curved knife and in her left a skull cup

46

filled with *amrita*, the nectar of immortality. We should visualize Vajrasattva not as though made of flesh and blood, but like a rainbow in the sky, vivid yet void. However, he is not just a physical appearance like a rainbow; he is pervaded by the wisdom and compassion of all the Buddhas. Think of him as your kind root teacher, appearing in the form of Vajrasattva.

The second strength is the strength of deep, intense remorse for our past actions. If you had swallowed a powerful poison without realizing it, you would certainly feel desperate when you found out you were going to die. Similarly, up to now we have not been aware of the accumulation of devastating power from the negative actions we have committed throughout many past lives. Today, realizing that the very cause of our wandering in samsara and of all our suffering is these negative actions, we feel a strong regret at having behaved so carelessly. If we did not feel this regret, we would just continue to accumulate negative actions and perpetuate our suffering; but now we realize that we need to purify ourselves, so we turn to Vajrasattva to request the means to do so.

Why is Vajrasattva the one we choose for this purification? When he vowed to achieve Enlightenment for the sake of all beings, he made this wish: "When I become a fully enlightened Buddha, may all beings be purified of their obscurations, their ignorance and their negative actions simply by hearing my name, seeing my form, remembering me, or reciting the mantra that contains my name."

Since regret alone is not enough, one must put into action the means for purifying oneself. This is done

47

through the strength of the antidote. Direct your whole mind towards Vajrasattva, confident that, since he is the all-encompassing sovereign of all mandalas, the union of all the Buddhas, he has the power to purify your obscurations. With Vajrasattva above your head as previously described, visualize, in his heart center, a moon disc upon which is a white letter HUNG, surrounded by the hundred-syllable mantra.

Recite:

Ah! On the crown of my head, on a lotus and a
moon,
Sit Guru Vajrasattva and consort.
From the mantra in his heart falls a stream of
nectar,
Which purifies illness, harmful influences, negative
actions and defilements.

Then recite the hundred-syllable mantra as many times as you can.

While reciting, generate strong devotion towards Vajrasattva, thinking, "Because of my past actions in this life and in all my previous lives, I am in this miserable situation in samsara. Grant your blessings now to purify me, or I will continue to circle in samsara forever."

Our fervent supplication, offered with hands folded and tears of devotion in our eyes, invokes the wisdom mind of Vajrasattva to purify our negative actions. By the power of our prayer, from the letter HUNG in his heart, luminous nectar, which contains all the wisdom, loving kindness and power of Vajrasattva starts to flow. This nectar completely fills the bodies of Vajrasattva and his consort and flows out from the point of their union, from their toes and from all the pores of their bodies. The stem of the thousand-petaled lotus upon which Vajrasattva sits, above the crown of our head, enters the Brahma aperture, the opening in the top of our head. The nectar flows down through this aperture and fills our body, completely washing away all our obscurations and impurities, which pour forth from all the pores and apertures of our body. Our sicknesses come out in the form of pus and blood; negative influences in the form of insects, scorpions, and snakes; and mental obscurations as dark, smoky liquid. The cleansing stream of nectar is extremely powerful, washing away all our obscurations in the same way that a flood carries away all the trees and rocks in a valley. As these obscurations flow out of our body, the earth below us opens, down to seven levels below the surface. There, in the form of a red bull with a gaping mouth, is Yama, Lord of Death. This dirty liquid enters his mouth, and turns into nectar as he swallows it. Now all our karmic debts, our past actions, have been transformed into wisdom, totally purified. Similarly, not only is our body purified, but even the ordinary aggregates and elements - our flesh, blood, bones and skin - are no longer gross material substances; they become transparent, as if made of light. We are completely clear and luminous inside and out. Then we think that this red bull, and all those to whom we have past karmic debts, are completely satisfied. The earth beneath us closes again and we are completely purified, our body pure and transparent like crystal.

The *amrita* from Vajrasattva still continues to flow down, progressively filling our body. As it fills our head, we receive the blessings of Vajrasattva's body, and all negative actions committed with our bodies, such as killing, stealing, and sexual misconduct, are purified; we receive the vase initiation and the seed is planted for realizing the *Nirmanakaya*, the manifested body of the Buddhas. When the nectar reaches our throat, we receive the blessings of Vajrasattva's speech, and all the negative actions committed through our speech, such as lies, idle speech, slander, and harsh words are purified; we receive the secret initiation and the seed is planted for realizing the *Sambhogakaya*, the body of perfect enjoyment. Then, as the nectar flows down to our heart level, we receive the blessings of Vajrasattva's mind, and all our negative thoughts, such as animosity, envy, and false views are purified; we receive the third empowerment, the wisdom initiation, and the seed is planted for realizing the *Dharmakaya*, the Absolute Body. Finally, as the nectar reaches our navel center, throughout our body we receive the fourth initiation, the initiation of word, which indicates the absolute nature; all the subtle defilements of body, speech and mind are purified, we receive the blessing of the adamantine wisdom of Vajrasattva, and the seed is planted for realizing the *Vajrakaya*, the unchanging adamantine body of all the Buddhas. Then we conclude by reciting the supplication to Vajrasattva, saying:

Protector, I have been ignorant and foolish, and I have broken and degenerated the samaya. Guru and protector, be my refuge! Sublime Vajra Holder, embodiment of great compassion, supreme among beings, I take refuge in you. I repent and confess all

*deteriorations, breaches, faults and downfalls of
root and branch samayas related to body, speech
and mind. Cleanse and purify all negative actions,
obscurations and habitual tendencies.*

As soon as we have said this, we think that not
only our own defilements and obscurations, but those
of all beings, are completely purified. Following our
supplication, Vajrasattva, very pleased, smiles and
says, "Noble child, you are now purified of all obscurations." After that say:

Vajrasattva melts into light and dissolves into me.

The moment Vajrasattva dissolves into us, we no
longer have our ordinary form, but become Vajrasattva, in union with his wisdom consort. In our heart
center is a white moon disc, upon which there is a blue
letter HUNG surrounded by the six-syllable mantra, OM
VAJRA SATVA HUNG (pronounced *om benzar sato hung* in Tibetan). In front, which we think of as being to the east,
there is the white syllable OM; on the right, or to the
south, are the yellow syllables VAJRA; behind, or to the
west, is the red syllable SAT; on our left, or to the north,
is the green syllable TVA.

Boundless rays of multicolored light emanate from
the HUNG, as well as from the syllables of the mantra, to
the Buddhafields of the ten directions, making infinite
offerings to the Buddhas and Bodhisattvas. We then
think that the Buddhas, having accepted our offerings,
send back their blessings, all their wisdom, loving
kindness, and power, in the form of rays of light which
dissolve into us. Like a lotus bud starting to bloom

51

when the rays of the sun fall upon it, Vajrasattva becomes even more brilliant and perfect.

Then we visualize that from our whole body and from the syllables of the mantra, boundless rays of light emanate, filling the universe around us. The universe is now no longer an ordinary impure place, but the perfect Buddhafield of Vajrasattva, the Buddhafield of Pure Joy. Sentient beings are also no longer ordinary; all the males have the form and nature of Vajrasattva, and all the females the form and nature of Vajratopa, the wisdom consort. To the east all beings become white Vajrasattvas and Vajratopas of the Adamantine or Vajra family; to the south they become yellow Vajrasattvas and Vajratopas of the Jewel or Ratna family; to the west, they become red Vajrasattvas and Vajratopas of the Lotus or Padma family; to the north they become green Vajrasattvas and Vajratopas of the Action or Karma family; and in the center, they become blue Vajrasattvas and Vajratopas of the Tathagata family. All these beings are continuously reciting the hundred-syllable mantra, the sound of which fills the whole of space.

In this way, appearances, sounds and thoughts are no longer ordinary, but appear as the sheer display of wisdom. The external world is a Buddhafield and beings in it are manifestations of Vajrasattva and Vajratopa, all sounds are the resonance of mantra and all thoughts are the spontaneous display of bliss-emptiness.

We then recite the six-syllable mantra as many times as we can. At the end of the session, the whole outer universe, together with the beings in it, starting

from the outside, dissolves into ourselves as Vajrasattva and consort. Then the consort dissolves into
Vajrasattva; Vajrasattva melts into light and dissolves
into the mantra in our heart center. The syllables of the
mantra dissolve into each other one by one and then
into the central letter HUNG. The HUNG, starting from the
bottom, dissolves upward, melting into light, until finally it vanishes like a rainbow in the sky, leaving only
the vast expanse of luminous voidness. Sit for a while,
simply remaining in that state of utter simplicity, free
from all concepts and clinging.

After a while, when we start to come out of this
meditation and thoughts again arise in our mind, we
should think that all outer appearances are a Buddhafield, all beings are deities, all sounds are mantras, and
all thoughts are wisdom. As the mirror of our mind has
been wiped clean through the Vajrasattva practice, the
nature of all phenomena appears clearly in it.

In order to make our purification enduring, we
must now apply the fourth strength, the strength of
promise. This means to have the unwavering determination that even at the cost of our life we will not rel-
apse again into negative actions, which, we now
know, are the cause of our suffering and what keeps
us circling in samsara.

To conclude, we make a deeply felt dedication of
the merit for the sake of all sentient beings, saying, "By
this merit, may all sentient beings swiftly achieve the
level of Vajrasattva himself," offering all the benefits
from this practice completely to all sentient beings. We
should not think that the merit is divided up among

them, but that each and every being receives all of the merit in its entirety.

When dedicating the merit, however, we should keep in mind that in absolute truth there is no one who dedicates, no object of dedication and no act of dedicating, thus remaining free of clinging and concepts.

Recite the hundred-syllable mantra 100,000 times and then the six-syllable mantra 600,000 times. Until you have completed the number of recitations of the hundred-syllable mantra, spend most of each practice session on that, and then recite the shorter mantra a few times at the end. When you have completed the recitation of the hundred-syllable mantra, recite it just a few times at the beginning of each session and then concentrate on the recitation of the shorter mantra.

We should remember that meditating upon Vajrasattva is the same as meditating upon all the Buddhas; to achieve the realization of Vajrasattva is to achieve the qualities of all the Buddhas. Moreover, the mantra of Vajrasattva, the hundred-syllable mantra, is the hundred peaceful and wrathful deities in the form of sound; it embodies all the wisdom and power of Vajrasattva himself. If we recite the hundred-syllable mantra twenty-one times every day, concentrating the mind totally on the visualization of the pouring down of nectar and the purification, there is no breach of any vow or samaya[8], and no obscuration that cannot be purified. If we recite the hundred-syllable mantra one hundred times without distraction, even what is called a "sin with immediate effect"[9] can readily be purified. If we do this practice, all the Buddhas will think of us as their own child and all the hindrances to our spiritual experience and ultimate realization will be dispelled.

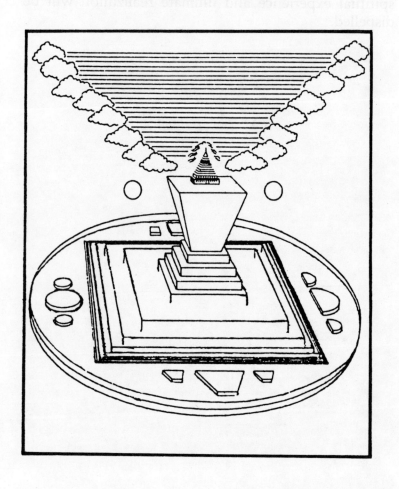

MANDALA OFFERING

Of all practices, the offering of the mandala is the most profound and skillful way to accumulate merit and wisdom, the provisions without which we cannot travel swiftly along the path.

If you develop a strong feeling of renunciation towards samsaric concerns, if you are constantly aware of impermanence and if you accumulate merit and wisdom, it will be quite easy to obtain true and direct realization of the Great Seal and the Great Perfection. Otherwise, if you say, "Merit is for the followers of the lower vehicles; I am only interested in practicing the Great Perfection," and sit staring at the sky, not thinking of impermanence or the defects of samsara, you will not have real endeavor, and genuine meditative experiences will not develop.

You may wish to progress in your spiritual experience and achieve ultimate realization through the Vajrayana path; but without accumulating merit and wisdom, you will not reach that goal. If you had prepared a magnificent feast, a king would be willing to attend; in the same way, if you prepare the feast of the twofold accumulation of merit and wisdom, the king of experiences and realization will enter your being.

To perfect this accumulation there are many methods, but the swiftest, and at the same time the easiest and most profound, is the offering of the whole universe in the form of a mandala.

According to different *ngondro* traditions, we make either a thirty-seven-fold offering or, as here, a seven-fold offering of the mandala of the universe. The seven-fold offering is the offering of Mt. Meru, the four continents, the sun and the moon. In the tradition of the Ancient Translations, the Nyingmapa, we also make the offering of the Three Kaya mandalas - the mandalas of the Dharmakaya, Sambhogakaya and Nirmanakaya.

When making the actual offering, we use a mandala plate, which symbolizes the golden ground of the universe. If one is wealthy, one may use a plate made of gold, silver or copper. If one is a humble practitioner living in a mountain retreat, one may use whatever one finds, such as a flat stone or a plank of wood. To symbolize the offering of the universe, we pour onto the plate grains - wheat, corn, peas or rice - in order to create the appropriate connections for all countries to enjoy prosperity and good crops. We offer medicinal grains and plants, like *arura* and *pharura*[10], in order to create the appropriate connections for dispelling epidemics and sicknesses in the world. We offer precious stones such as amber, pearls, gold, silver, coral and turquoise, in order to create the appropriate connections for the wealth of our meditative experiences and realization to increase.

We usually use two mandala plates; one, placed upon the shrine, symbolizes the object of refuge, to whom we make the offering. The other, held in the hand, symbolizes the universe that we are offering. When we use rice or any other kind of grain, the grain must be washed very carefully and cleared of all stones, pieces of wood and dirt. It is then washed in saffron water and dried in a clean place; the grain is now ready to be offered.

Hold the mandala plate in the left hand. With the right hand, put a drop of saffron water upon the plate, and holding a pinch of grain between the thumb and ring finger, clean the mandala plate with a clockwise circular motion of the heel of the hand, while reciting the hundred-syllable mantra, wishing, "May all my obscurations and those of all sentient beings be purified." One may also recite the Mantra of Perfect Discipline[11] in order to purify oneself before making the offering.

For the offering itself we recite the *Offering of the Three-Kaya Mandala*, offering seven heaps of grain each time.

OM AH HUNG

I offer the Buddhafields of the Three Kayas, riches,
And clouds of offerings, outer, inner and secret,
To the Three Jewels and the Three Roots.
Accepting them, grant the supreme and common
*   accomplishments.*

OM AH HUNG GURU DEWA DAKINI SAPARIWARA
RATNA MANDALA PUJA MEGHA AH HUNG.

The Nirmanakaya mandala

One begins by first offering the mandala of Nirmanakaya, the body of manifestation. This is a symbolic offering of the universe, with Mount Meru at its center; in the east, the continent Purvavideha, made of pure crystal; in the south, our continent, Jambud-vipa, made of blue sapphire; in the west, the continent Aparagodaniya, made of red ruby; and in the north, the continent Uttarakuru, made of gold. The four faces of Mount Meru are made of the same precious sub-stances as each of the continents facing them. The sky in each continent is given its color by the substance particular to it. So the sky is white over the eastern continent, blue over our continent, red over the west and yellow over the north. Each of these continents has one subcontinent on either side. The eastern con-tinent has Deha and Videha; our southern continent has Camara and Aparacamara; the western continent has Shatha and Uttaramantrina, and the northern con-tinent has Kuruva and Kaurava. Altogether that makes twelve continents and subcontinents. On the four con-tinents, east, south, west and north, are the mountain of jewels, the wish-fulfilling tree, the bountiful cow and the spontaneous crop. There are also the seven emblems of royalty[12], the treasure vase, and the eight offering goddesses. In the east is the sun, and in the west the moon.

Within, on, and above Mount Meru are the six realms of the world of desire, the seventeen levels of the world of form, and the four levels of the world of formlessness. In the celestial realms are lakes of pure nectar, wish-fulfilling trees, mountains of gold and jewels, and beautiful gardens and forests. Around Mount Meru are seven ranges of golden mountains, separated by seven oceans. At the periphery is a circle of blazing iron mountains. We make the offering of the whole universe as if we were its owner, the univer-sal monarch. This vast offering includes all the perfect, beautiful and precious things that can be found in the universe - below, upon and above the earth - such as the wish-fulfilling gem of the nagas, which sheds light throughout the naga world in the depths of the great oceans.

We practice the mandala offering in order to be able to give without clinging. At present, we have strong attachments to what we possess. We cannot bear to give our possessions away and sometimes do not even dare make use of them ourselves, out of fear that they may get used up or spoiled. So in order to cut through clinging and attachment to material things, we offer to the Buddhas and Bodhisattvas all that we have, our possessions, our good qualities, our knowledge and all the merits we have accumulated in the past. We do not only offer the little we have in this life; we make a limitless offering, the entire system of the universe - and not only our own universe, but a billion universes. All this we offer to the object of refuge for the benefit of all beings, and especially for those whom we consider our enemies, those who are creating difficulties and obstacles for us. We pray that through the merit of this practice these beings will be led on to the path of liberation and ultimately achieve Buddhahood. Unless we have this attitude, our practice is not genuine Mahayana practice.

The Sambhogakaya mandala

Above the Nirmanakaya mandala, we visualize and offer the Sambhogakaya mandala, the body of perfect enjoyment, which is the offering of the Buddhafields of the five Buddha families. We visualize these five Buddhafields high above us in the sky. In the center is the Densely Arrayed Buddhafield of the Buddha Vairocana. In the east is the Buddhafield of Pure Joy of the Buddha Akshobhya. In the south is the Utterly Beautiful Buddhafield of the Buddha Ratnasambhava. In the west is the Blissful Buddhafield of the Buddha Amitabha, and in the north is the Buddhafield of Totally Fulfilled Action of the Buddha Amoghasiddhi.

The Dharmakaya mandala

Thirdly, we offer the all-pervading Dharmakaya mandala, which is our realization of the absolute nature, without any concept whatsoever of a subject who offers, an object to whom offering is made, or an act of offering. To relate this symbolically to the structure of the other mandalas, we can consider that the universally void nature is the ground of the mandala, while the qualities of Buddhahood, such as the four fearlessnesses, the ten powers and the eighteen correct discriminations, correspond to the different elements of the universe offered in an ordinary mandala.

The text that one recites begins with the three syllables OM AH HUNG, which symbolize the wisdom body, speech and mind and, as well, the Three Kayas of the Buddhas. The body corresponds to the Nirmanakaya, the speech to the Sambhogakaya and the mind to the Dharmakaya. The Dharmakaya is the absolute nature of the Buddhas; the Sambhogakaya is the five wisdoms that emanate from this nature; and the Nirmanakaya is the all-encompassing compassion of the Buddhas which manifests in whatever way is beneficial to sentient beings.

The outer offerings are cleansing water, flowers, incense, light, perfume, food, music and so forth, as well as the offerings of the five senses - all that is perceived and enjoyed through sight, hearing, smell, taste and touch. The inner offerings are amrita, rakta and torma, as well as various sacred substances which serve to repair and fulfill the samaya promises and to bring blessings. The secret offerings are those made by the sixteen offering goddesses.

The recipients of our offerings are the Three Jewels and the Three Roots. Having accepted these offerings, they grant us their blessings in return. They accept our offering out of great compassion and joy, seeing that through accepting it they grant us the means to complete our accumulation of merit and wisdom and thus to free ourselves from samsara.

The mantra that concludes the verse of offering opens with OM AH HUNG, the three syllables that represent the body, speech and mind of the Buddhas, the Three Roots and the Three Kayas. GURU, or *Lama* in Tibetan, refers to all the spiritual teachers of the lineage; DEWA or *Lha* refers to the yidam deities; DAKINI or *Khandro*, refers to the feminine principle of the Buddhas. The first is the root of blessings, the second is the root of accomplishment, the third is the root of activity. SAPARIWARA means 'together with their retinue'; RATNA means 'jewel'; MANDALA is the mandala of the universe; puja means 'offering', and MEGHA means 'cloud'. AH multiplies the offering infinitely, and HUNG requests the

Three Jewels and the Three Roots to accept our offering and grant us their blessings in return.

We make this offering and recite the lines that accompany it 100,000 times. Instead of the verses quoted above, we may recite, if we prefer, the four line verse commonly used when requesting teachings and expressing gratitude for them. These lines are found both in Guru Padmasambhava's *Stages of the Path of the Secret Mantras* and in Lord Atisha's *Stages of the Path*:

> *The ground is purified with scented water and strewn with flowers,*
> *It is adorned with Mount Meru, the four continents, and the sun and moon.*
> *Thinking of it as a blessed Buddhafield, I offer it*
> *So that all beings may enjoy the happiness of the perfectly pure Buddhafields.*

We can also use the more elaborate recitation of the thirty-sevenfold mandala, which was composed by the great Sakyapa teacher, Drogön Phakpa, the Noble Protector of Beings. The text we choose depends upon how elaborate we want our offering to be.

At the end of the session of offering, think that the Buddhas and Bodhisattvas of the ten directions of space have accepted your offering and have granted the means of progressing on the path to ultimate realization.

The three supreme methods

The framework which gives this practice - as well as any other practice or activity we undertake - its strength, is the "three supreme methods": the preparation, in which we generate Bodhicitta, the wish to act and practice for the sake of all beings; the actual practice, during which we remain free of distractions, clinging and concepts; and the conclusion, in which we dedicate the merit for the sake of all beings. These three methods must be applied to any kind of practice, whether Development Stage, Completion Stage, Great Seal, Great Middle Path, or Great Perfection. Without these three supreme methods, it is quite useless to do any practice.

The preparation is the generation of Bodhicitta, which acts as skillful means for one's practice. Why do we say "skillful means"? In modern technology, very powerful machines are used which in one hour can do the same work that it would take a hundred people to accomplish by hand. That is what is meant by skillful means. Likewise, if we undertake an action with the pure intention of benefiting others, that is the skillful means which makes this action infinitely beneficial and efficient. Of body, speech and mind, by far the most important in determining the quality of an action is the mind. So when starting a practice, we first must turn our minds inwards and check our intention.

The correct way to think is this: "Of all living beings there is not a single one who has not been my parent in a past life. Now they are all immersed in the ocean of suffering. They all want happiness, but do not know how to bring it about. I wish to help them, but do not have the ability to do so. I must therefore progress towards enlightenment, so as to gain the ability to free all sentient beings from their suffering and ignorance."

All actions one does must be approached in this way, even those that seem insignificant, like reciting a single *mani*, or going once around a temple or a stupa. Do everything with the thought, "May it be for the sake of all beings." To recite OM MANI PADME HUNG even once brings boundless merit; it will close the doors to the lower realms and lead to the Buddhafields. But if that single recitation of the *mani* is reinforced with the attitude of Bodhicitta, its benefit will increase continuously throughout many lives. The reason for this is that if we dedicate an action for the sake of all beings, just as the number of beings is infinite, so also will the benefit of that action be infinite. To recite a hundred million *manis* without dedicating them to the welfare of all beings would be of far less benefit than to recite just a hundred manis for the sake of all beings.

The main part, the actual practice, must be free of concepts and clingings. Ideally, this means to have full realization of emptiness, the void nature of phenomena. But this is something that is not easily understood at the beginning, so for us the main point is to be fully concentrated on the practice with body, speech and mind working in harmony. For instance, if we do prostrations with the body whilst carrying on an ordinary conversation and our mind is full of thoughts of attachment and hatred, the body is only making mechanical and rather useless movements. Instead, we should always combine body, speech and mind in our practice. With the body we prostrate, with the speech we recite the refuge prayer, and with the mind we remain concentrated on the meaning of doing those prostrations. We must remember that when we place our folded hands at our forehead, we pay homage to the body of the Buddhas. When we place them at our throat, we pay homage to their speech, and when we place them at our heart, we pay homage to their mind. Then, when we touch the ground with our forehead, two hands and two knees, we pay homage to the body, speech, mind, qualities, and actions of the Buddhas; and at the same time the five poisons that all beings, including ourselves, have in our minds, are transformed into the Five Wisdoms. This is the kind of precise mindfulness that one should maintain. Even in daily life, a good worker is someone who is always mindful in his action. With his body he is concentrated on his work; with his speech he discusses what has to be done and what needs to be avoided; and with his mind he thinks very carefully about the job he is doing. Otherwise one might end up like the tailor who was always looking out of the window and chatting to whoever was in the workshop while he was sewing - he found he had stitched the garment he was making to his own clothes.

When we say that the actual practice must be "free from concepts and clingings," it means free from attachment, from self-infatuation, from scattering thoughts and so forth. If we make a vast offering, such as ten thousand silver coins, we should not think, "Oh! I made such a big offering! That is enough for the rest of my life. I am going to reap the fruit of my actions, enjoy their karmic result. In fact, I probably made the biggest offering ever made by anyone." An offering made with such a small-minded attitude is in fact very limited and quite useless. We should wish that our offering could be multiplied without limit. If we offer one million, we should wish to be able to offer two, and at the same time remain free of pride. There are four ways to waste a generous action: to hope for a reward, to boast to others about it, to regret having done it, and to omit dedicating its merit to all beings. In brief, a good action must be completely free from any kind of second thoughts and expectations and, ideally, should be free of the concepts of a doer, an object and an action.

When we practice, our mind must be free of poisonous thoughts, or we will spoil the whole thing, like mixing delicious food with poison. In the same way, if we intend to do a positive practice with the body, speech and mind but we adulterate it with thoughts of attachment, anger and pride, our practice will not be of much benefit. If we are able to purify our body, speech and mind together, we will become like immaculate cloth perfectly cut and stitched, or like a precious stone, a diamond or a sapphire, without the slightest irregularity or flaw.

The third of the three supreme methods, the conclusion, is the dedication of merit, which will make the fruit of this merit continue to increase, instead of being exhausted as soon as it is enjoyed. Whether we have done one or a thousand prostrations, or offered one or a thousand butter-lamps, we should pray, "I dedicate the merit of this offering I have made, representing all the positive actions I have done in the past, am doing now, and shall do in the future, for the sake of all sentient beings throughout space, especially those whom I perceive as my enemies." When we make this dedication we should be very clear about what we are doing, as if we were handing over a present to each and every living being. We should not think that this merit is shared out among all sentient beings, but that each and every being gets the full amount of it.

If we associate these three supreme methods with any action, even if it is not such an obviously vast action as reciting hundreds of millions of mantras or offering huge sums of money, it will have boundless, true benefit.

It is because of Bodhicitta, the pure and vast intention, that the Great Vehicle, the Mahayana, is called "great". Without Bodhicitta, we might call ourselves practitioners of the *Great* Perfection, the *Great* Seal or the *Great* Middle Path, but we would still be on the narrow path of selfishness.

If we have these three supreme methods, we have everything we need. If we do not have them, there is no way to progress. Genuine practice is something that has to be developed. We have to transform ourselves; if, right from the beginning, we were completely free from attachment and anger and constantly had the infinite number of sentient beings in mind, we would already be realized and would have no need to practice in the first place. But this is not the case. This is why we need to be mindful of the meaning of the teachings and vigilant in watching the actions of our body, speech and mind. If we practice in this way, we will progress along the path without much difficulty. It is like a child who has been well brought up; we can see from his behavior - how he eats and so forth - that his mind has been changed by this training.

We must be able to retain in daily life the understanding we have found in meditation. Otherwise we may think we have reached a high level, but actually we will stumble on the first obstacle we meet, and we will not be able to deal with the various circumstances encountered in daily life. Meditation and post-meditation periods should reinforce and complement each other, otherwise it will be hard to achieve liberation.

In the beginning it is not very easy; in the middle it is not very stable; in the end it becomes very natural. For this reason, it is at the beginning that we must apply the strongest endeavor and diligence. Please think carefully about this.

71

GURU YOGA

In the so-called preliminary, or foundation practice, the most extraordinary part is Guru Yoga, or "union with the Guru's nature", the practice through which primordial wisdom can arise instantly in one's being.

Guru Yoga is the way to pray to an authentic teacher and express one's deep and unchanging devotion. Through devotion, one's mind and the Guru's mind become one. Why is this practice necessary? There is not a single Buddha in the past, present or future who achieved or will achieve enlightenment without having relied upon a spiritual teacher. Whichever of the nine vehicles of the Buddhist teachings one practices, one must rely upon a spiritual teacher, receive his teaching and practice according to his instructions. There is no other way.

Yet, even if one has met a teacher and received his instructions, unless one has fervent devotion and complete confidence in him and in his teachings, one will never receive his blessings; and without this blessing one will not progress along the path. So, first of all, one needs to generate devotion.

At the beginning, devotion does not flow spontaneously, so we need to generate and cultivate it in our mind. In order to generate devotion, first, when we hear about the teacher's life, we think about his amazing enlightened qualities. Then, when we meet him, we see that those qualities are real and genuine, and progressively our confidence and faith grow stronger and stronger. We start to pray to him from deeper and deeper within, and his blessings begin to penetrate us more and more deeply.

All accomplishments are due to the Guru's blessings. By accomplishments we do not mean achieving things like good health, long life or wealth. These are minor accomplishments. We mean the supreme realization of the enlightened nature of the Guru, which is also our own Buddha nature.

The visualization

The actual text we use to help us generate devotion says:

> Before me in the sky, in an expanse of rainbow
>   light,
> Is my root teacher, Pema Thödrengtsal,
> Surrounded by the ocean of Knowledge Holders of
>   the three transmissions.
> He is the union of all objects of refuge.

Here we visualize our root teacher in the form of Guru Rinpoche; but we may also visualize him in the form of Vajradhara, or as we usually see him. The main point is to visualize whoever inspires in us the strongest and most spontaneous devotion.

Imagine that the place where you are is no longer an ordinary place, but the Glorious Copper-Colored Mountain, Sangdopalri, Guru Rinpoche's Buddhafield.

In the middle of this Buddhafield, in which everything is made of jewels and precious substances, is the immeasurable Palace of Lotus Light, made of pure light - transparent and filled with rainbows. We ourselves are not in our ordinary form, but that of Vajrayogini. She stands in the center of the palace, upon a lotus, sun disc and corpse. She is red, bright as a ruby, brilliant as the sun. She is peaceful, standing, in a dancing posture, on her left leg, with her right leg drawn up. She wears the silk, jewels and bone ornaments of the Sambhogakaya deities. In her right hand, she holds a curved knife, which symbolizes cutting through ego-clinging; and in her left, a skull cup filled with amrita, the nectar of immortality. In the crook of her left arm, resting upon her shoulder, is the *khatvanga*, which represents Guru Rinpoche in a hidden form. She is dancing beautifully and peacefully. She has a most compassionate expression and at the same time she displays her sharp canines in a slightly wrathful smile, which symbolizes her victory over delusion. Her form is that of Vajrayogini; her nature is that of the supreme consort, Yeshe Tsogyal, the Queen of the Ocean of Wisdom.

Above our heads, in a mass of rainbow light, is the Lotus-Born Guru, as Pema Thodrengtsal. We visualize him very clearly, not made of gross material substances like a statue, or flat like a thangka painting, but transparent, vivid and clear. We should visualize even the most minute details, like the black and white of his eyes and the golden designs upon the brocade of his robe. He is transparent, like a rainbow, but not just a visual image, for he is permeated with the wisdom, compassion and power of all the Buddhas of the three times and the ten directions of space.

He is sitting on a throne supported by eight fearless lions. Upon the throne rests a lotus and sun and moon discs. For the details of the visualization, we can refer to a painting or image of Guru Rinpoche.

Guru Rinpoche himself promised, "Whoever meditates upon me meditates upon all the Sugatas." Through Guru Rinpoche, we receive all the blessings of all the Buddhas and Bodhisattvas; and, in particular, to pray to Guru Rinpoche as being inseparable from our own root teacher is the surest way to receive boundless blessings. Simply by praying to our root teacher, we will gather the blessings of all the Buddhas, Manjushri, Avalokiteshvara, Vajrapani and so forth, just as a gutter collects all the rainwater that falls upon a roof. The Guru himself is the sovereign of all mandalas, the lord who embodies outwardly the Three Jewels (Buddha, Dharma and Sangha), inwardly the Three Roots (Guru, Yidam and Dakini), and secretly the Three Kayas (Dharmakaya, Sambhogakaya and Nirmanakaya).

Devotion

The most important point is to have devotion. Guru Rinpoche said, "I am present in front of whoever has faith." So, simply through our having strong faith, the blessings and presence of Guru Rinpoche, of our Guru and of all the Buddhas will be with us at all times. When we pray to Guru Rinpoche, visualizing him above our heads, we should not think that through our prayer Guru Rinpoche will appear sometime in the future and bless us. We should think that because of our devotion he is truly present, right now, with all his wisdom and compassion. Guru Rinpoche himself said, "Give me your heart and mind. I will always be near you."

There are many prayers we can use as a support for our devotion. Among them is one known as the Seven-Line Prayer. This is the prayer that the dakinis used when they requested Guru Rinpoche to arise from the *dharmadhatu*, the absolute expanse, and manifest in this world for the sake of all beings. It is the prayer that one finds in every sadhana of Guru Rinpoche, hidden by Guru Rinpoche himself as *terma*, or spiritual treasure, for the sake of future generations. It is said that just as a mother cannot resist responding when her child calls her, so too Guru Rinpoche will come from the glorious Copper-colored Mountain to anyone who chants the Seven-Line Prayer:

> *HUNG!*
>
> *On the northwest border of the land of Oddiyana,*
> *On the pollen bed of a lotus,*
> *You who have attained the wondrous supreme*
>   *siddhi*
> *Are renowned as the Lotus Born,*
> *Surrounded by a circle of many dakinis.*
> *Following after you, I will practice;*
> *I beseech you, come and grant your blessings.*
>
> *GURU PEMA SIDDHI HUNG*

Our devotion must be such that our Guru is always present in our minds. Whether we are happy or we suffer, whether we encounter good or ill, we will have no other object of hope, no reliance other than him. If we meet with wealth, comfort and other agreeable circumstances, we should realize that comforts and wealth have no essential reality; they have come to us simply as the blessings of our teacher. We should offer them to the teacher as a mandala, and make use of them to benefit other beings and the teachings.

At times of suffering, sickness, slander and persistent difficulties, we should be grateful that, through the blessings of the Guru, we can experience these sufferings now, when we have a way to purify them. We should think, "This is just the consequence of having harmed others in my past lives and of having committed all sorts of negative actions. If I do not purify these actions now, my fate can only be to take rebirth in the lower realms in many future lives. By the kindness of my teacher, I am now able to purify my karma. I pray that through my experience of this suffering, all similar sufferings that afflict other beings may be exhausted through mine." Thus, in happiness we should not feel proud; in difficulties, we should not feel discouraged. At all times we should keep our mind unwaveringly turned towards the Guru.

When we say we should think of nothing but the Guru, this means that when we walk, we visualize the Guru sitting above our right shoulder and we are moving as if we were circumambulating him with great respect. When we sit, we visualize the Guru above our head. When we eat, we visualize the Guru in our throat and we offer the first and best part of the food to him. When we rest at night, we visualize the Guru in the center of our heart, seated on a four-petaled red lotus and radiating light that fills the whole universe. When we have the Guru always in mind and think of nothing but him, even if we experience great sadness or discomfort of mind, the simple fact of remembering the Guru completely clears away all of these difficulties and fills our mind with joy and confidence.

The Vajra Guru mantra

After the Seven-Line Prayer, recite the twelve-syllable mantra of Guru Padmasambhava. This mantra is the quintessence of the twelve branches of the Buddha's entire teaching. The twelve syllables of the mantra purify the twelve interdependent links, which perpetuate ignorance and suffering; they recall the twelve deeds displayed by Guru Rinpoche during the time of his manifestation in this universe. This is not only a mantra addressed to Guru Rinpoche, but includes the Three Jewels, the Three Roots, and the infinite number of peaceful and wrathful Buddhas.

OM AH HUNG, the first three syllables of the mantra, stand for the three aspects of Guru Rinpoche corresponding to the Three Kayas - the Buddha Amitabha, the Dharmakaya; Avalokiteshvara, the Sambhogakaya; and Padmasambhava, the Nirmanakaya. VAJRA indicates the unchanging, adamantine wisdom of Guru Rinpoche. GURU means "heavy" in Sanskrit and refers to the enormous weight of the teacher's qualities. It also refers to the weight of the benefit derived from following his instructions and of the harm created for oneself and others by not following them. PEMA or lotus refers to Guru Rinpoche's name and to his immaculate birth upon the pollen bed of a lotus flower. SIDDHI refers to the common and supreme accomplishments, and HUNG is a call to Guru Rinpoche, requesting him to bestow these accomplishments upon us.

Recite the Seven-Line Prayer 100,000 times and the mantra 1,300,000 times (a number which corresponds to 100,000 for each of the twelve syllables plus 100,000 more to compensate for any defects in the recitation). Or, if one wishes to do the recitation in a briefer way, one may recite the mantra 400,000 times.

Above all, Guru Yoga is the most profound of practices, and yet presents no dangers or risks. It does not involve complex and difficult visualizations, as in the mandalas of the Development Stage. It has none of the risks involved in meditating upon the channels, energies, and inner heat of the Completion Stage. At the same time, if one practices Guru Yoga correctly, all the qualities of the Development and Completion Stages will naturally arise. Conversely, without devotion to the Guru, even if one practices the Development and Completion Stages for years, one's practice will never be firm and one will never taste its fruit. As Jigme Lingpa said, "To have confidence in the teacher is the ultimate refuge."

Receiving the four empowerments

After having recited the Seven-Line Prayer and
Guru Rinpoche's mantra, we receive the blessings of
his Body, Speech, Mind, and Wisdom through rays of
light emanating from his three centers and his whole
body. The letter om in his forehead center emanates
white light which is absorbed into a corresponding
om in our forehead, and which purifies the negative
actions of the body. Similarly, the letter AH in his throat
center emanates red light to purify negative actions of
speech; and the letter HUNG in his heart center emanates blue light to purify negative actions of the
mind. Finally his whole body emanates five-colored
rays of light - white, red, blue, yellow and green -
which are absorbed throughout our bodies, purifying
all of our subtle obscurations related to body, speech
and mind. Simultaneously we receive the four empowerments or *abishekas*: the vase, secret, wisdom and
symbolic empowerments, which sow in our beings the
seeds of realization of the four Kayas. The text says:

> *Through the light rays from the three seed-sylla-*
> *bles at the three places*
> *I obtain blessings, empowerments and accomplish-*
> *ments.*
> *The Guru melts into light and dissolves into my-*
> *self.*
> *Inseparable from him, rest in simplicity.*

At the end, the Guru above our head melts into a mass of light, which in turn dissolves into us. We think that our mind and the Guru's mind are mingled inseparably. Then we too dissolve into light and remain in a state of utter simplicity, the absolute nature of mind. When thoughts arise again, we should perceive the phenomena of forms, sounds and recollections as the display of the Guru's body, speech and mind. All forms are the manifestation of the Guru's body; all speech and sounds are the Guru's speech and the natural resonance of the twelve-syllable mantra; and all thoughts are the play of the Guru's mind - no longer deluded thoughts, but the natural creativity of awareness, the nonconceptual wisdom that is the nature of Guru Rinpoche's enlightened mind. The fact that, when looking at the mind, one cannot ascribe to it any color, shape, or location is the void aspect of the mind. That it can perceive and know all phenomena of samsara and nirvana is its clarity aspect.

Conclusion

We must combine our strong devotion and yearning with the wish to benefit all sentient beings. When we pray to the teacher we should think that all sentient beings are praying together with us, as if we were leading the prayer. When we receive the blessings of Guru Rinpoche, we must think that all sentient beings are receiving it with us. At all times we should pray to the teacher, knowing that it is more beneficial and precious for our progress towards enlightenment to offer even a single drop of scented oil to our teacher's body than to fill the whole of space with offerings to the Buddhas of the ten directions.

At the end, we should dedicate the merit of this practice to all sentient beings, so that they may meet Guru Rinpoche himself, hear his voice, realize his wisdom, and be reborn as soon as they die in the Pure Land of the Glorious Copper-Colored Mountain. There, meeting Guru Rinpoche in person, may they complete the rest of the path towards Buddhahood.

Guru Yoga must be at the center of our practice from the very moment we have entered the door of the Dharma until we achieve the ultimate realization of Ati Yoga or Great Perfection. In brief, Guru Yoga is the most efficient way to progress along the path and to dispel any obstacles confronting us. This is why we should make it the center of our practice and keep it in the core of our hearts at all times.

This concludes the explanation of this short *ngondro* practice composed by Jamyang Khyentse Wangpo. A more detailed explanation of the *ngondro* practice can be found in Patrul Rinpoche's *Kunzang Lamai Shelung*[13].

These teachings were given at Shechen Tennyi Dargyeling Monastery, Kathmandu, Nepal, over six days in December 1987, by H.H. Dilgo Khyentse Rinpoche, at the request of the Sawang Urgyen Osel Mukpo and numerous disciples wishing to practice the ngondro.

Translated by Konchog Tenzin. Transcribed and edited by Nur and Shirin Gale, Suzan Garner, Tim Olmsted, Ani Ngawang Chodron, Larry Mermelstein, Charles Hastings and John Canti.

We would like to thank Tony Duff, of the Nalanda Translation Committee, for preparing the typesetting used to reproduce this text and for his precious technical advice.

Clifford Leeb, Wulstan Fletcher, Christian Bruyat and Kunzang Chödron kindly read this text before publication and offered their suggestions.

Finally, we express our gratitude to Erik Pema Kunzang who published this book, and to the generous benefactor who made this *publication possible.*

NOTES

1. Bardo: The intermediate state between death and the next life.

2. The three worlds of samsara: the worlds of desire, of form and of formlessness.

3. The five silken garments are: the ribbons hanging from the diadem, the scarves for dance, the shoulder shirt, the skirt, and the belt.

4. The eight jeweled ornaments are: diadem, earings, three rows of necklaces, arm bracelets, wrist bracelets, and anklets.

5. This point is rarely understood by western students. Yet, to step over a book, whether it may be a holy scripture or not, is a transgression of the refuge vows. One should even avoid walking on anything written on the ground.

6. Respectively the Great Seal and the Great Perfection.

7. *Vajratopa* (Skt.), rdo-rje snyems-ma (Tib.)

8. *Samaya:* the sacred bond which the disciple has formed with his teacher.

9. There are five sins with immediate effects, which means that, at the time of death, one will immediately be drawn to the lower states of existence without even going through the experiences of the *bardo*, the intermediate state: (1) to kill one's father, (2) to kill one's mother, (3) to kill an Arhat, (4) to draw blood from the body of a Buddha with an evil intention, and (5) to cause a schism within the spiritual community.

NOTES

10. Arura is myrobalan (Lat. *Terminalia chebula*,) the universal medicinal plant. Pharura is *Terminalia Belerica* (Lat.)

11. The mantra of perfect discipline is pronounced *Om Amogashila Sambhara Sambhara Bhara Bhara Mahashudha Sato Pema Bibhukshite Bhudza Dhara Dhara Samantha Avalokite Hung Phet Soha.*

12. The seven emblems owned by a *Chakravartin,* a universal monarch. These and the eight offering goddesses are listed in the thirty-seven-fold mandala prayer which can be found in the appendix.

13. The *Kunzang Lamai Shelung* has been translated into French under the title *Le Chemin de la Grande Perfection,* (Editions Padmakara 1987). An English translation is at present nearing completion. For an extensive teaching on Guru Yoga by H.H.Dilgo Khyentse Rinpoche, see *The Wish-Fulfilling Jewel,* (Shambala 1988).

TEXT AND OUTLINE
OF THE PRELIMINARY
PRACTICE

ༀ། །བླ་མ་མཁྱེན་ནོ། །ལན་གསུམ།

LAMA KYENO!
Lama Kyeno!

[Recite three or more times, with the visualization described on page 1]

THE SIX CONTEMPLATIONS

[Then reflect upon the six contemplations explained from pages 2 to 17. When beginning the full ngondro practice, spend one, three, seven, or more days reflecting on each topic until the meaning remains vividly present in your thoughts. Later on, always start the practice by reflecting upon these six topics]

ད་ལྟ་འབྱོར་རྙེད་དཀའ་དོན་ཆེན་ཐོབ་དུས་འདིར། །

DAL JOR NYE KA DÖN CHEN THOB DU DHIR
Now that I possess these freedoms and endowments, so difficult to obtain, and of such importance,

སྣོད་བཅུད་མི་རྟག་དྲན་པས་རྒྱུད་བསྐུལ་ནས། །

NÖ CHU MITAK DRENPE GYU KUL NE
May I arouse my mind by remembering the impermanence of the universe and beings.

སྲིད་གསུམ་སྡུག་བསྔལ་མཚོ་ལས་ངེས་འབྱུང་ཕྱིར། །

SI SUM DUG-NGEL TSO LE NGE JUNG CHIR
To free myself truly from the ocean of suffering of the Three Worlds,

བླང་དོར་མ་ནོར་ལམ་ལ་བརྩོན་ནུས་ཤོག །   ཅེས་མངྒ་ལས་སོ། །

LANG DOR MA NOR LAM LA TSÖN NU SHO
Without confusing what is to be adopted and what is to be abandoned, may I persevere in the path.

(Those four lines were written by Mangala, Dilgo Khyentse Rinpoche)

TAKING REFUGE

[Visualize the assembly of the object of Refuge following the explanations given on p. 19 to 28, and do full prostrations while reciting the four lines below which combine the Refuge and Bodhicitta vow. 100,000 prostrations should be done accompanied by the same number of recitations of the following.]

ན་མོ། བདག་སོགས་འགྲོ་ཀུན་བྱང་ཆུབ་བར། །

NAMO DA SO DRO KUN CHANG CHUB BAR
Homage! Until the enlightenment of myself and all beings,

རྩ་བ་གསུམ་ལ་སྐྱབས་སུ་མཆི། །

TSAWA SUM LA KYAB SU CHI
I take refuge in the Three Roots.

གཞན་དོན་སངས་རྒྱས་འཐོབ་བྱའི་ཕྱིར། །

SHEN DÖN SANG GYE THOB CHE CHIR
To obtain Buddhahood for the benefit of others,

སྨོན་འཇུག་དོན་དམ་བྱང་སེམས་བསྐྱེད། །

MÖN JUK DÖN DAM CHANG SEM KYE
I generate Bodhicitta, as aspiration, as action, and in its absolute meaning.

[Dissolve the visualization as explained p. 24 and share the merits]

BODHICITTA PRACTICE

[Start by reflecting briefly upon the six topics, and recite the verse of taking Refuge three times. Then concentrate on the Bodhicitta practice itself. Visualize the refuge assembly as witness, and again recite 100,000 times the four lines above, this time focusing on relative and absolute Bodhicitta as explained from p. 29 to 42.]

VAJRASATTVA PRACTICE

[Start the practice by going briefly through the previous steps of the ngondro. Then, following the explanations given on pp. 45 to 55, visualize Vajrasattva and recite the hundred-syllable mantra.]

ཨ༔ བདག་ཉིད་སྤྱི་བོར་པད་ཟླའི་སྟེང་། །

A DA NYI CHIWOR PE DE TENG
A! On the crown of my head, on a lotus and moon,

 བླ་མ་རྡོ་རྗེ་སེམས་མ་ཡབ་ཡུམ་གྱི། །

LAMA DORSEM YAB YUM GYI
Sit Guru Vajrasattva and consort.

ཕུག་ས་ཀའི་སྔགས་ལས་བདུད་རྩིའི་རྒྱུན། །

THUK KE NGAK LE DUTSI GYUN
From the mantra in his heart falls a stream of nectar,

བབས་པས་ནད་གདོན་སྡིག་སྒྲིབ་སྦྱངདས། །

BAP PE NE DÖN DIK DRIP JANG
Which purifies illness, harmful influences, negative actions and defilements.

[Recite the hundred-syllable mantra (Appendix 1)

At the end of the session, recite the confession prayer (Appendix 2) and say:]

རྡོར་སེམས་འོད་ཞུ་རང་ལ་ཐིམ། །

DORSEM Ö SHU RANG LA THIM
Vajrasattva melts into light and dissolves into me.

[Visualizing yourself as Vajrasattva, as described on pp. 48 to 51, recite the six-syllable mantra (Appendix 3).

First recite the hundred-syllable mantra 100,000 times, reciting the six-syllable mantra 108 times at the end of each session. When 100,000 recitations of the hundred-syllable mantra have been completed, start the session by reciting the hundred-syllable mantra 21 or 108 times and then concentrate on repeating the six-syllable mantra 600,000 times, with the corresponding visualization.]

OFFERING OF THE MANDALA

*[Start each session by going through the previous steps of the ngondro, then visualize the assembly of those to whom you are making the offering. Recite the thirty-seven-fold mandala offering (**Appendix 4**) once or more, and then, following the explanations given on pp. 57 to 63, concentrate upon reciting the verse and mantra below 100,000 times, each time pouring seven heaps of rice onto the mandala plate. As explained in the main teaching, one may substitute here the four-line mandala offering given in **Appendix 5**]*

ཨོཾ་ཨཿཿ་ཧཱུྃ།

OM AH HUNG

རྐུ་གསུམ་ཞིང་ཁམས་ལོངས་སྤྱོད་དང་། །

KU SUM SHING KHAM LONG CHÖ DANG
I offer the Buddhafields of the Three Kayas, riches,

ཕྱི་ནང་གསང་བའི་མཆོད་པའི་སྤྲིན། །

CHI NANG SANG WE CHÖPE TRIN
And clouds of offerings, outer, inner and secret,

དཀོན་མཆོག་རྩ་བ་གསུམ་ལ་འབུལ།།

KONCHOK TSAWA SUM LA BUL
To the Three Jewels and the Three Roots.

94

 བཞེས་ནས་མཆོག་ཐུན་དངོས་གྲུབ་སྩོལ།།

SHE NE CHOK THUN NGÖDRUP TSÖL
Accepting them, grant the supreme and common accomplishments.

ༀ་ཨཱཿཧཱུྃ་གུ་རུ་དེ་བ་ཌཱ་ཀི་ནི་སཔ་རི་ཝཱ་ར་
རཏྣ་མཎྜལ་པཱུ་ཛ་མེ་གྷ་ཨཱཿཧཱུྃ༔

OM AH HUNG GURU DEWA DAKINI SAPARI-
WARA RATNA MANDALA PUJA MEGHA AH
HUNG.

[At the end of the practice, dissolve the visualization and share the merit.]

GURU YOGA

After having gone briefly through the previous sections of the ngondro, concentrate on the visualization and recitation of the Guru yoga following the explanations given on pp. 73 to 84]

རང་མདུན་ནམ་མཁར་འཇའ་འོད་ཀློང་། །

RANG DUN NAMKHAR JA Ö LONG
Before me in the sky, in an expanse of rainbow light

རྩ་བའི་བླ་མ་ཐོད་ཕྲེང་རྩལ། །

TSAWE LAMA THÖDRENGTSAL
Is my root teacher, Pema Thödrengtsal,

བརྒྱུད་གསུམ་རིག་འཛིན་རྒྱ་མཚོ་སྐོར། །

GYU SUM RIGDZIN GYAMTSÖ KOR
Surrounded by the ocean of Knowledge Holders of the three transmissions,

སྐྱབས་ཀུན་འདུས་པའི་ངོ་བོར་བཞུགས། །

KHYAP KUN DUPE NGOWOR SHUK
He is the union of all objects of refuge.

ཚིག་བདུན་གསོལ་འདེབས་དང་བསྙེན་པ་བཟོག་ཏུ་ལའབད།

Earnestly recite the seven-line prayer and the "Vajra Guru" mantra.

[First complete 100,000 recitations of the seven-line prayer, *(Appendix 6), concluding each session by reciting the Vajra Guru mantra (Appendix 7) a few hundred times, and receiving the four empowerments as below. When the above number has been completed, begin the session by reciting the seven-line prayer 7 or 21 times and concentrate on reciting the Vajra Guru mantra 1,300,000 times.*

མཐར།

At the end of each session receive the four empowerments and dissolve the visualization]

གནས་གསུམ་འབྲུ་གསུམ་འོད་ཟེར་གྱིས། །

NE SUM DRU SUM ÖZER KYI
Through the light rays from the three seed-syllables at the three places

བྱིན་རླབས་དབང་དང་དངོས་གྲུབ་ཐོབ། །

CHIN LAP WANG DANG NGÖRUP THOP
I obtain blessings, empowerments and accomplishments.

བླ་མ་འོད་ཞུ་རང་ལ་ཐིམ།།

LAMA Ö SHU RANG LA THIM
The Guru melts into lights and dissolves into myself.

དབྱེར་མེད་མ་བཅོས་ལྷུག་པ་པར་བཞག། །   དགེ་བ་བསྔོ།།

YERME MACHÖ LHUKPAR SHAK
Inseparable from him, rest in simplicity.

Dedicate the merits.

ཞེས་པ་འདང་མཁྱེན་བརྩེའི་དབང་པོས་སོ།།

This was written by Khyentse Wangpo

1) THE HUNDRED-SYLLABLE MANTRA

ༀབཛྲ་སཏྭ་སམཡ༔ མ་ནུ་པཱ་ལ་ཡ༔

OM BENZAR SATTO SAMAYA MANUPALAYA

བཛྲ་སཏྭ་ཏྲེ་ནོ་པ་ཏི་ཥྛ༔ དྲྀ་ཌྷོ་མེ་བྷ་ཝ༔

BENZAR SATTO TENOPATICH'TRA DRIDHRO ME BHAWA

སུ་ཏོ་ཥྱོ་མེ་བྷ་ཝ༔ སུ་པོ་ཥྱོ་མེ་བྷ་ཝ༔

SUTOKAYO ME BHAWA SUPOKAYO ME BHAWA

ཨ་ནུ་རཀྟོ་མེ་བྷ་ཝ༔ སརྦ་སིདྡྷི་མྨེ་པྲ་ཡཙྪ༔

ANURAKTO ME BHAWA SARWA SIDDHIM ME PRAYATSA

སརྦ་ཀརྨ་སུ་ཙ་མེ༔ ཙིཏྟཾ་ཤྲཱི་ཡཾ༔ ཀུ་རུ་ཧཱུྃ༔

SARWA KARMA SUTSA ME TSITTAM SHRIYAM KURU HUNG

ཧ་ཧ་ཧ་ཧ་ཧོཿ བྷ་ག་ཝཱན་སརྦ་ཏ་ཐཱ་ག་ཏ

HA HA HA HA HO BHAGAWAN SARWA TATHAGATA

བཛྲ་མ་མེ་མུ་ཙུ་བཛྲི་བྷ་ཝ་

BENZAR MAME MUNTSA BENZI BHAWA

མ་ཧཱ་སམ་ཡ་ས་ཏྭ་ཨཱཿ

MAHA SAMAYA SATTO AH

2) THE CONFESSION PRAYER

མགོན་པོ་བདག་ནི་མི་ཤེས་རྨོངས་པ་ཡི། །

GONPO DA NI MI SHE MONGPA YI
Protector, I have been ignorant and foolish

དམ་ཚིག་ལས་ནི་འགལ་ཞིང་ཉམས། །

DAMTSIK LE NI GAL SHING NYAM
And broken and degenerated the samaya.

བླ་མ་མགོན་པོས་སྐྱབས་མཛོད་ཅིག །

LAMA GONPO KHYAP DZÖ CHIK
Guru and protector, be my refuge!

གཙོ་བོ་རྡོ་རྗེ་འཛིན་པ་སྟེ། །

TSOWO DORJE DZINPA TE
Sublime Vajra Holder,

ཐུགས་རྗེ་ཆེན་པོའི་བདག་ཉིད་ཅན། །

THUKJE CHENPO DANYI CHEN
Embodiment of great compassion,

འགྲོ་བའི་གཙོ་ལ་བདག་སྐྱབས་མཆི། །

DRO WE TSO LA DA KHYAP CHI
Supreme among beings, I take refuge in you.

སྐུ་གསུང་ཐུགས་དང་རྩ་བ་ཡན་ལག་གི་དམ་ཚིག །
ཉེས་ལྟུང་ཐམས་ཅད་མཐོལ་ལ་ཞིང་བ་བཤགས་སོ། །

KU SUNG THUK DANG TSAWA YENLAK GI
DAMTSIK NYE TUNG THAMCHE THOL SHING
SHAKSO
I repent and confess all deteriorations, breaches, faults
and downfalls of the root and branch samayas related
to body, speech and mind.

སྡིག་སྒྲིབ་བག་ཆགས་དྲི་མའི་ཚོགས་རྣམས་བྱང་
ཞིང་དག་པར་མཛད་དུ་གསོལ། །

DIK DRIP PAK CHAK TRIME TSO LE NAM CHANG
SHING DAKPAR DZE TU SÖL
Cleanse and purify all negative actions, obscurations
and habitual tendencies.

3) THE SIX-SYLLABLE MANTRA

ཨོཾ་བཛྲ་སཏྭ་ཧཱུྃ།

OM BENZAR SATTO HUNG

4) THE OFFERING OF THE THIRTY-SEVENFOLD MANDALA

ཨོཾ་བཛྲ་བྷུ་མི་ཨཱཿཧཱུྃ།

OM BENZAR BHUMI AH HUNG
[*The Vajra ground*]

གཞི་ཡོངས་སུ་དག་པ་དབང་ཆེན་གསེར་གྱི་ས་གཞི།

SHI YONG SU DAKPA WANG CHEN SER KYI SA SHI
The foundation is the utterly pure golden ground of vast strength,

ཨོཾ་བཛྲ་རེ་ཁེ་ཨཱཿཧཱུྃ།

OM BENZAR REKHE AH HUNG
[*The Vajra fence*]

ཕྱི་ལྕགས་རི་འབོར་ཡུག་གིས་བསྐོར་བའི་དབུས་སུ་ཧཱུྃ།

CHI CHAK RI KHOR YUG KI KHOR WE U SU HUNG
**The boundary is a ring of iron mountains encircling the
syllable Hung.**

རིའི་རྒྱལ་པོ་རི་རབ།

RI'I GYALPO RIRAP
Here are Sumeru, king of mountains, [In the center]

ཤར་ལུས་འཕགས་པོ།

SHAR LU PHAKPO
In the East, Purvavideha,

ལྷོ་འཛམ་བུ་གླིང་།

LHO DZAMBU LING
In the South, Jambudvipa,

ནུབ་བ་ལང་སྤྱོད།

NUP BALANG CHÖ
In the West, Aparagodaniya,

བྱང་སྒྲ་མི་སྙན།

CHANG DRA MINYEN
In the North, Uttarakuru.

ཁྱུས་དང་ལྱུས་འཕགས།

LU DANG LU PHAK
Deha and Videha, *[Toward the East]*

རྔ་ཡབ་དང་རྔ་ཡབ་གཞན།

NGAYAP DANG NGAYAP SHEN
Camara and Aparacamara, *[Toward the South]*

གཡོ་ལྡན་དང་ལམ་མཆོག་འགྲོ།

YÖ DEN DANGLAM CHOK DRO
Satha and Uttaramantrina, *[Toward the West]*

སྒྲ་མི་སྙན་དང་སྒྲ་མི་སྙན་གྱི་ཟླ།

DRA MINYEN DANG DRA MINYEN GI DA
Kurava and Kaurava *[Toward the North]*

རིན་པོ་ཆེའི་རི་བོ།

RINPOCHE RIWO
The Jewel Mountain,

དཔག་བསམ་གྱི་ཤིང་།

PAKSAM KYI SHING
The Wish-Fulfilling Tree,

 འདོད་འཇོའི་བ།

DÖ JÖ'I BA
The Bountiful Cow,

མ་མོ་ས་པའི་ལོ་ཏོག།

MAMÖ PE LOTOK
And the Spontaneous Harvest.

འཁོར་ལོ་རིན་པོ་ཆེ།

KHORLO RINPOCHE
The Precious Wheel,

ནོར་བུ་རིན་པོ་ཆེ།

NORBU RINPOCHE
The Precious Jewel,

བཅུན་མོ་རིན་པོ་ཆེ།

TSUNMO RINPOCHE
The Precious Queen,

བློན་པོ་རིན་པོ་ཆེ།

LÖNPO RINPOCHE
The Precious Minister,

ब्लूर་པོ་རིན་པོ་ཆེ།

LANGPO RINPOCHE
The Precious Elephant,

རྟ་མཆོག་རིན་པོ་ཆེ།

TACHOK RINPOCHE
The Precious Horse,

དམག་དཔོན་རིན་པོ་ཆེ།

MAPÖN RINPOCHE
The Precious General,

གཏེར་ཆེན་པོའི་བུམ་པ།

TERCHEN PÖ'I BUMPA
And the vase of great treasure.

སྒེག་པ་མ།

GEKPA MA
The Lady of Charm,

ཕྲེང་བ་མ།

TRENGWA MA
The Lady of Garlands,

སྒྱུ་མ།

LU MA
The Lady of Song,

གར་མ།

GAR MA
The Lady of Dance,

མེ་ཏོག་མ།

METOK MA
The Lady of Flowers,

བདུག་སྤོས་མ།

DUPÖ MA
The Lady of Incense,

སྣང་གསལ་མ།

NANGSEL MA
The Lady of Light,

དྲི་ཆབ་མ།

TRICHAP MA
The Lady of Perfume.

ཉི་མ།

NYIMA
The Sun

ཟླ་བ།

DAWA
And the Moon.

རིན་པོ་ཆེའི་གདུགས།

RINPOCHE'I DUK
The Jeweled Canopy,

ཕྱོགས་ལས་རྣམ་པར་རྒྱལ་བའི་རྒྱལ་མཚན།

CHOKLE NAMPAR GYALWE GYALTSEN
And the Banner of Universal Victory.

ལྷ་དང་མིའི་དཔལ་འབྱོར་ཕུན་སུམ་ཚོགས་པ་
ཚང་བ་མེད་པ་འདི་ཉིད་རྩ་བ་དང་བརྒྱུད་པར་བཅས་
པའི་དཔལ་ལྡན་བླ་མ་དམ་པ་རྣམས་དང་ཡི་དམ་འཁྱིལ་
འཁོར་གྱི་ལྷ་ཚོགས་སངས་རྒྱས་དང་བྱང་ཆུབ་སེམས་
དཔའི་ཚོགས་དང་བཅས་པ་རྣམས་ལ་དབུལ་བར་བགྱིའོ།།

LHA DANG MI'I PALJOR PHUNSUM TSOKPA
MATSANGWA MEPA DI NYI TSA WA DANG

GYUPAR CHEPE PALDEN LAMA DAMPA NAM
DANG YIDAM KHYIL KHOR KYI LHA TSOK SANGYE
DANG CHANGCHUP SEMPE TSOK DANG CHEPA
NAM LA BUL WAR GYI'O
The glory, wealth, and enjoyments of gods and men,
with nothing lacking - all this I offer to the glorious
holy root master and the masters of the lineage, to the
herukas, and the host of deities of the mandala and to
the assembly of the Buddhas and Bodhisattvas.

ཐུགས་རྗེས་འགྲོ་བའི་དོན་དུ་བཞེས་སུ་གསོལ།

THUKJE DROWE DÖN DU SHE SU SÖL
Accept it with compassion for the benefit of beings;

བཞེས་ནས་བྱིན་གྱིས་བརླབ་ཏུ་གསོལ།

SHE NE CHIN KYI LAP DU SÖL
Having accepted it grant your blessing.

5) THE SHORT MANDALA OFFERING

ས་གཞི་སྤོས་ཀྱིས་ཆུག་ཤིང་མེ་ཏོག་བཀྲམ།

SA SHI PÖ KYI CHUK SHING METOK TRAM
The ground is perfumed with scented water and strewn
with flowers.

རི་རབ་གླིང་བཞིའི་ཉི་ཟླས་བརྒྱན་པ་འདི། །

RI RAP LING SHI NYI DE GYENPA DI
Adorned with Mount Meru, the four continents, the sun and the moon.

སངས་རྒྱས་ཞིང་དུ་དམིགས་ཏེ་ཕུལ་ཡི་ས། །

SANGYE SHING TU MIKTE BULWA YI
Imagining this as a Buddhafield, I offer it

འགྲོ་ཀུན་རྣམ་དག་ཞིང་ལ་སྤྱོད་པར་ཤོག །

DRO KUN NAMDAK SHING LA CHÖPAR SHO
So that all beings may enjoy that pure realm.

ཨི་དམ་རཏྣ་མཎྜལ་ཀཾ་ནིརྻ་ཏ་ཡ་མི།

IDAM RATNA MANDALA KAM NIRYATA YAMI

6) THE SEVEN LINE PRAYER

ཧཱུྃཿ

Hung!

ཨོ་རྒྱན་ཡུལ་གྱི་ནུབ་བྱང་མཚམསཿ

HUNG ORGYEN YUL KYI NUB CHANG TSAM
On the north-west border of the land of Oddiyana,

པདྨ་གེ་སར་སྡོང་པོ་ལཿ

PEMA KESAR DONGPO LA
On the pollen bed of a lotus,

ཡ་མཚན་མཆོག་གི་དངོས་གྲུབ་བརྙེསཿ

YAMTSEN CHOK GI NGÖDRUP NYE
You who have attained the wondrous supreme siddhis,

པདྨ་འབྱུང་གནས་ཞེས་སུ་གྲགསཿ

PEMA JUNGNE SHESU TRA
Are renowned as the Lotus Born,

འཁོར་དུ་མཁའ་འགྲོ་མང་པོས་བསྐོརཿ

KHOR DU KHANDRO MANGPÖ KOR
Surrounded by a circle of many dakinis.

110

ཁྱེད་ཀྱི་རྗེས་སུ་བདག་སྒྲུབ་ཀྱིས༔

KHYE KYI JESU DA DRUP KYI
Following after you, I will practice;

བྱིན་གྱིས་རློབས་ཕྱིར་གཤེགས་སུ་གསོལ༔

CHIN KYI LOP CHIR SHEK SU SOL
I beseech you; come and grant your blessings.

གུ་རུ་པདྨ་སིདྡྷི་ཧཱུྃ༔

GURU PEMA SIDDHI HUNG.

7) THE VAJRA GURU MANTRA

ༀ་ཨཱཿཧཱུྃ་བཛྲ་གུ་རུ་པདྨ་སིདྡྷི་ཧཱུྃ༔ .

OM AH HUNG VAJRA GURU PEMA SIDDHI HUNG